Loving Someone Who Has Sexual Trauma

A Compassionate Guide To Supporting Your Partner & Improving Your Relationship

Megan Lara Negendank, LMFT, CST

16pt

Copyright Page from the Original Book

Publisher's Note

This publication is designed to provide accurate and authoritative information in regard to the subject matter covered. It is sold with the understanding that the publisher is not engaged in rendering psychological, financial, legal, or other professional services. If expert assistance or counseling is needed, the services of a competent professional should be sought.

NEW HARBINGER PUBLICATIONS is a registered trademark of New Harbinger Publications, Inc.

New Harbinger Publications is an employee-owned company.

Copyright © 2023 by Megan Negendank
New Harbinger Publications, Inc.
5720 Shattuck Avenue
Oakland, CA 94609
www.newharbinger.com

All Rights Reserved

Acquired by Wendy Millstine

Edited by Rona Bernstein

Library of Congress Cataloging-in-Publication Data on file

TABLE OF CONTENTS

Foreword	v
Introduction	ix
CHAPTER 1: Understanding Your Partner and the Survivor Experience	1
CHAPTER 2: Impact of Sexual Trauma on Your Relationship	47
CHAPTER 3: Your Relationship as a Source for Healing	100
CHAPTER 4: Using Relationship Skills to Create a Secure Connection	133
CHAPTER 5: Coping with Trauma Triggers	163
CHAPTER 6: Establishing (or Regaining) Intimate Connection and Pleasure	195
CHAPTER 7: Stages of Healing and Hope for the Future	229
Acknowledgments	257
References	259
Back Cover Material	265

"Megan has shed light, compassion, and hope on a sorely under-discussed topic: how to best support a partner with a sexual trauma history. As a fellow trauma therapist, I deeply respect the way Megan has approached this topic with a wonderful combination of psychoeducation, coping skills, and stories to equip partners of those who have experienced sexual trauma to both show up for them and for themselves."

—**Annie Wright, LMFT,** licensed psychotherapist, relational trauma recovery specialist, and trauma therapy center founder

"Although resources for survivors of sexual trauma abound, very few exist for their intimate partners. Partners play a crucial role in the day-to-day lives, sexual experiences, and healing journeys of survivors. It can be difficult to understand reactions and coping mechanisms a survivor may express. To know what to say or how to react. Negendank's work is a pivotal asset in helping alleviate relationship distress while increasing intimacy and pleasure."

—**Natasha Helfer, LCMFT, CST-S,** group practice director at Symmetry Solutions, host of the *Natasha Helfer Podcast,* and director of religion and mental health treatment at the Buehler Institute

"Megan's approach is validating and compassionate. The couples' stories she shares are relatable, inclusive, and cover a broad range of how people and relationships are impacted by the ripple effects of sexual trauma. Her book creates space for self-reflection and personal growth, and it offers practical strategies you can begin implementing right away, all while feeling like Megan is right there with you guiding you through your own healing process."

>—**Ivy Griffin, LMFT, CAMFT Certified Supervisor,** owner/director of Thrive Therapy & Counseling, a team of therapists specializing with highly sensitive people and trauma

"Negendank has delivered a practical guide filled with prompts, applications, and succinct psychoeducation surrounding the realities of sexual trauma and how it exists in and around us. Her words provide empathy, compassion, and support for readers across the board."

>—**Ashley Rakela, LMFT,** relational art therapist for individuals, couples, and families in private practice

"Megan's warmth, wealth of experience, grounding in research, and authentic voice make *Loving Someone Who Has Sexual Trauma* an essential and accessible resource for all those who want to help create healing spaces for survivors of sexual trauma."

—**Susan DuBay, MA, LMFT,** internal family systems trauma psychotherapist working in private practice with individuals and couples

"Finally, a compassionate, realistic, and helpful guide in supporting our intimate partners healing from sexual trauma! So much individual healing happens through our relationships, and yet, there has been a void of resources supporting partners of survivors navigating this part of the journey. As a therapist who has been waiting for practical and accessible support like this, I cannot wait to share this book with my clients!"

—**Maegan Tanner, MA, AMFT, APCC,** therapist working in private practice with individuals and couples

"Sexual trauma survivors and their partners often face the aftermath of trauma and abuse alone. *Loving Someone Who Has Sexual Trauma* offers a new path toward hope and healing. With warmth and experience, Megan guides partners of sexual trauma survivors in supporting themselves, their partner, and their relationship."

—**Daylyn Musante, LCSW,** licensed psychotherapist specializing in relationship therapy for couples and individuals

The Loving Someone Series

If your loved one has a psychological disorder, you want to do everything you can to help them feel loved, supported, and safe. However, it's also important for you to establish personal boundaries so that you can avoid becoming overwhelmed.

New Harbinger's *Loving Someone Series* was developed to help readers like you truly understand a loved one's disorder, the medication or treatments that are available, and how to take care of your own needs so that you don't lose yourself in the process. As the family member or partner of someone with mental illness, you face your own set of unique challenges. Our books can provide powerful, evidence-based tools to help both you and your loved one live happier, healthier lives.

For a complete list of books in this series, visit newharbinger.com

Foreword

If you are the partner of someone who has survived sexual trauma, your relationship has undoubtedly created an array of conflicting feelings, from love and passion to confusion, hurt, and anger. The fact is, no matter how much you may love your partner, it can at times be difficult to understand why they act as they do, even years after the traumatic event first occurred. Your partner seems to be on a roller coaster, but when you try to help, nothing you do seems right. Your relationship with a survivor of sexual trauma can leave you feeling exhausted and questioning your self-worth. You may spend so much time supporting your partner that you feel lost yourself, unsure of who you are and what more you can do.

Fortunately, you have chosen to read *Loving Someone Who Has Sexual Trauma*, a compassionate and encouraging book by my colleague Megan Negendank. In a straightforward but gentle way, Negendank explains not only the effects of sexual trauma on your partner so that you can understand why they react as they do, but also the effect of their trauma symptoms on *you*. While many books have been written for the person suffering with PTSD and other impacts of trauma, little practical help has been available for the partner navigating the late effects of sexual trauma until now.

While Negendank acknowledges that being the partner of someone who has experienced sexual trauma can be difficult, even exhausting, it also presents an opportunity for understanding and growth. Once you understand the behaviors of your partner, you still need to know how to respond. Often the impulse is to rush in and fix things, and while sometimes your efforts are welcome, other times you find yourself being pushed away. Or because you're not sure quite what to do to comfort your partner, you decide to give them some space—and then find out that what they really wanted was attention. You can end up feeling pulled every which way, with a bubbling cauldron of different feelings. And here's the thing—that's what your partner is feeling, too. Then the two of you are stuck in the cauldron!

But it doesn't have to be that way. Fortunately, there are solutions and tools you can use to manage yourself and manage your relationship—including letting go of the urge to manage your partner and make things all better, a challenging task for anyone. By reading these pages, you'll understand your partner's specific symptoms and why they've persisted. You'll learn to build trust that may have been eroded, even if you are trustworthy, and why consent, even in a committed relationship, matters to your partner. You'll find out about the role of attachment in creating a safe, secure relationship not only for your partner's benefit, but also for your own.

You'll learn how it is possible to cope with trauma by reading the stories of all kinds of couples who have been there. You'll see how survivors and their partners have healed by engaging in easily adopted self-soothing practices like deep breathing and stress management. You'll read about how they also did deep inner work, reflecting on the nature of trauma and its impact. To help with this inner work, so necessary to healing, Negendank has included many questions, asking you to think about the situations of the couples she's presented, your own situation, and what will be helpful to you and your partner in creating a mutually nurturing bond.

Perhaps without realizing it, you will be learning life skills that can help you cope not only with the fallout of sexual trauma, but also with many stressful life situations. You'll become more self-compassionate and more resilient, which includes asking for help for yourself or your relationship if you need it. Negendank provides an outline of how to identify and discuss difficult topics, including, for example, how to bring up to your partner the possibility of being assessed for medications.

One of the biggest challenges for survivors of sexual trauma and their partners is establishing and maintaining a safe, healthy, and mutually fulfilling sexual relationship. For that reason, Negendank, who is an expert sex therapist, has included a chapter on intimacy and sexuality after trauma. Whether you read this chapter alone or with your partner, you will find out how to establish a feeling of safety so that you and your partner can be more open in your communication about sex. Such communication can include how you might create a joint vision of what you'd like your sex life to be like, or what sexual activities each of you enjoys or doesn't enjoy. You'll expand your idea of what constitutes "sex" too, so that you will have more opportunities for pleasure than when you were focused on a limited sexual script.

In short, the book you are holding is packed with an incredible amount of valuable and practical information that is paced in such a way that you can take your time and absorb what you are learning. You'll take better care of yourself and you'll find out that, ironically, in so doing you will be a better partner. You also may come to find that you have your own trauma—maybe not to the alarming level that your partner has experienced—that you have never dealt with because you didn't know how. With this book, you'll understand the nature of sexual trauma, and with Negendank's help, you'll know that it is possible, truly possible, to heal.

—Stephanie Buehler, MPW, PsyD, CST-S,
IF

Director, LearnSexTherapy.com
by The Buehler Institute

Introduction

Sexual trauma impacts far more people than those who experience it firsthand; it impacts the people who love and care about them too. Whether your partner's sexual trauma was days, months, or years ago, whether it was one horrible experience or many, your partner may have varying levels of trauma symptoms, and their relationships with friends, family members, and intimate partners may be impacted. This likely is what led you to this book.

After years in practice providing psychotherapy to individuals and couples who have been impacted by sexual trauma, I've noticed that the partners of sexual trauma survivors are often confused about how to help or what to say. Does this sound familiar? You may become overwhelmed or have a hard time understanding your partner's strong emotional reactions and behaviors. You may not know how to respond and feel like anything you say or do makes it worse.

It is hard to see someone we love in great distress—you may feel many of the same emotions your partner has experienced: shock, guilt, anger, fear, denial, grief. You may even experience vicarious trauma, which we will explore in chapter 2 of this book. Taking care of yourself and understanding the impact of this trauma on you and your relationship is a very important part of this book.

What I hope for you and anyone impacted by sexual trauma is to know that you are not alone. In our society, often just talking about sex or trauma can feel taboo—it's hard being open about events that have affected us deeply, and we may fear being judged by others or misunderstood when we do.

So, how do we get support in this area—especially when it can feel like an awkward topic to bring up with even our most trusted loved ones—and still protect the privacy of our partner? You may have found yourself googling for answers. You might even have found some good tips. What may have been sorely lacking in your research, though, are real stories. How are other partners of survivors coping? How are relationships really impacted when one or both partners are survivors of sexual assault? How do you support your partner in their healing while also having space to have your own needs met in the relationship? Is what you are experiencing normal?

Every day in my psychotherapy practice, I support survivors and their partners to heal through their trauma and find ways to trust intimate emotional and physical connection. One of the most common experiences of survivors and their partners is feeling alone with their pain. Sexual trauma isn't a rare experience, but it is not something we tend to discuss openly with others. This adds to a feeling of isolation and confusion, which can put additional stress on the relationship. By reading this book, you will learn about the many ways that sexual trauma can impact not only the survivor, but also their partner and the relationship itself—including future intimate relationships. Know that you are not alone, and that there are ways through the pain to a place of healing and connection.

Sexual trauma is extremely prevalent in our society. According to the National Sexual Violence Resource Center (2018), across the United States, about one in five women experience attempted or completed rape within their lifetime. In addition to this, just over 80% of women and just over 40% of men experience some type of sexual assault or harassment in their lives. So even though living with sexual trauma and supporting someone who does can feel lonely and isolating, far too many people in our society have experienced this trauma.

This book is organized into seven chapters. In chapter 1, we will learn more about the impact of the sexual trauma on your partner and read examples of survivor stories to help you see how sexual trauma impacts people and relationships differently. You'll likely recognize some of your own or your partner's experiences in these stories. In chapter 2, we will look more deeply at the impact of the sexual trauma on you and your relationship. Sexual trauma has a ripple effect on all people and areas of the survivor's life, and you will learn more about the pain you might be experiencing in your relationship. In chapter 3, you will learn how, through attachment science, your relationship offers great healing to you and your partner. We'll also look at ways you can decrease you own stress when you step into the role of helping your partner heal. In chapter 4, you will learn relationship skills that can help you now and for the rest of your life. In chapter 5, you will learn how to move through the most distressing moments in your relationship—when your partner experiences a trigger related to their trauma and you both become distressed. In chapter 6, you'll learn how to create a sexually satisfying relationship when one or both partners are survivors of sexual trauma. And finally, in chapter 7, you will hear from real survivors and their partners and undoubtedly walk away with hope for the future.

    Throughout this book, you will come across reflection questions and exercises to help you integrate information and skills you learn throughout your reading. I recommend that you have a dedicated journal for this purpose, but if you aren't the journaling type, it's not necessary. Additionally, there are several free tools, including worksheets, available on the website for this book, http://www.newharbinger.com/51574. (Seethe very back of this book for more details.) the very back of this book for more details.)

When I started working with sexual trauma survivors in my practice, I was initially surprised at how many partners wanted to come into a session to learn more about how to support their loved one. Survivors can feel so alone in their pain, but time and time again their partners walked into my office wanting to open up about their experiences and learn to be a better partner. As a survivor myself, I know how meaningful it is for another person to really see the pain we're in and want to help instead of running away. It's in these moments that I have hope for all of us.

By picking up this book, you are that person today: hoping to help your partner, hoping to help yourself, hoping to feel better in your relationship, and maybe ... hoping to change the world a little bit in doing so. Let's get started—you don't have to go it alone.

CHAPTER 1

Understanding Your Partner and the Survivor Experience

As a partner of someone who has experienced sexual trauma, you may feel myriad emotions, likely including uncertainly about how to help—and sometimes even how to *be*—in this relationship. This chapter will focus on laying the groundwork for how you can best support your partner, take care of yourself, and become closer in your relationship. Before we can do these things, it is helpful to understand what sexual trauma is, how common it is, and ways that your partner may have been affected by their trauma. Your role in this chapter is to read, understand, reflect, and gain more insight into your partner's experience.

You and Your Partner Are Not Alone

Below you will find five stories of partners navigating sexual trauma and the impact on their relationship. Themes and experiences included in these stories are common in my psychotherapy practice, but no story is based entirely upon or representative of a past or former client. These stories are an amalgamation of more than a decade of professional work and decades of personal experience and allyship. We will return to these survivor stories throughout the book.

• *Thomas and Marina*

Thomas (he/him) and Marina (she/her) have been married for five years. They met in their early twenties while working together at a restaurant.

Marina was raised in a high-conflict home. Her father abused alcohol and had a temper; her mom focused much of her time on keeping the household running and wasn't emotionally available. As a result, it was often hard for Marina to feel loved or open up to others and to trust that they'd care for her. Prior to meeting Thomas, Marina had a two-year serious dating relationship. This relationship was emotionally and sexually abusive; her partner did not respect Marina's boundaries and often pressured her into sex or became angry and threatening when she was not in the mood. When Marina met Thomas, she felt safer with him than with any man she had known in her life. Their friendship and partnership grew deeply and quickly.

Thomas loves feeling like Marina's protector. She is kind, funny, and beautiful. He loves feeling close to her emotionally and physically. In fact, being close to Marina is when he feels more secure and at ease than he's ever felt before.

After being married a few years, Thomas and Marina decided to become parents. Marina's pregnancy was mostly smooth, which was a relief to her, and Thomas felt tremendous joy when their baby was born. However, Marina has been very anxious since having the baby, and they're both navigating the stress of new parenthood. Thomas misses having time with Marina and often asks her why they don't find the time to talk with each other anymore, and why she never wants to have sex when he makes a move.

As for Marina, she finds herself shutting down and pulling away from Thomas. She tells him she feels pressured by him; she seems angry at him. She also feels guilty when she turns Thomas down, knowing he's confused and hurt. Finally, Marina opens up and shares about her past sexually and emotionally violent relationship. She tells Thomas he's triggering those memories for her and she doesn't know what to do. Thomas is hurt and defensive. He feels he's been nothing but supportive and loving to Marina; he misses connection with her, and he's offended that Marina is comparing him to her jerk ex-boyfriend. In the end, it feels like they don't understand each other anymore and Thomas is terrified he is losing his best friend and partner.

What parts of Marina and Thomas's story did you identify with? Why do you think Marina is feeling triggered right now and what might she need from Thomas? Why do you think Thomas is hurting and what do you think he wants Marina to understand?

• *Favor and Frank*

Favor (he/him) and Frank (he/him) have been in a monogamous relationship for three years. They have the same circle of friends and enjoy many of the same hobbies. Favor loves Frank's sense of humor, compassion, and ability to coordinate their social calendar. Frank finds Favor extremely attractive and intelligent and admires how dedicated he is to his career.

Favor and Frank's sexual relationship has been hot and heavy from the start. Their sexual attraction and chemistry were strong on their first date; they found connecting in this way easy and enjoyable. Bonding over so many shared interests also made dating and getting to know each other fun. They had nothing but high hopes for their relationship, and committing to a life together came naturally.

Recently, Favor has been taking on more responsibilities at work. He is much more stressed than normal, and when he's stressed he can pull away or seem grumpy. He's canceled plans with friends more than a few times, and Frank feels like he never sees Favor anymore. They are bickering often and end up having their first blow-up argument, which ends with Favor sleeping on the couch.

The next morning, Favor is feeling sheepish and wants to make it up to Frank. He slips back into bed during the early hours and begins rubbing Frank's upper leg, usually a mutually enjoyable move that ends in pleasurable sex for both. This time, though, Frank's body gets tense, and his breathing is fast and intense. He seems scared, and Favor stops immediately, realizing that Frank isn't fully there. They are quiet for a few stressful minutes before Frank bursts into tears. He tells Favor he does not want to talk about it, and he takes a shower. He avoids Favor the rest of the day.

Favor is worried, confused, and wants to know what he did wrong. He doesn't bring it up again, but asks Frank if he can talk about what happened via a text message. Frank says he's ready to talk about it tonight.

Frank opens up to Favor for the first time about a date rape he experienced five years ago. He is shaking as he shares. He feels embarrassed that the rape happened—he's never talked about it before and he's ashamed that he flashed to the rape when Favor made a move. He knows Favor didn't mean to hurt him, and he shares that he thinks he had a *panic attack. He also shares that he sometimes has nightmares about the rape but that he hasn't been triggered during sex before.*

Both partners are worried. Favor wants to support Frank and doesn't want to trigger him again. He's so afraid he's going to do something wrong. Frank feels guilty that his burden is now affecting their relationship. He doesn't want to lose Favor, but doesn't know what to do.

As you read Favor and Frank's story, do you identify with any parts? Why do you think Frank responded the way he did to Favor's touch? How do you think Favor is feeling and what might he want Frank to understand?

• *Gia and Samantha*

Gia (she/her) and Samantha (she/her) met seven years ago in a statistics class in college. They studied together and fell in love over quantitative analysis and laughing about the funny blouses their professor wore. After graduation, they moved in together. They adopted two rescued dogs and about a hundred houseplants. They love hosting book club for their friends and cooking delicious meals from scratch.

They understand that relationships have conflict and require work. They balance their time together and individual time exploring their own interests. They work on communicating honestly and respectfully to each other. They are both satisfied with their sex life and after seven years together, they understand the ebbs and flows of sexual connection.

Recently, Gia was sexually assaulted by an administrator, Theo, at the hospital where she works. Theo is her supervisor's boss. He had taken a special interest in Gia recently and offered to mentor her. She was excited for the opportunity and had been meeting with the administrator about twice a month for lunch and mentorship in his office.

He had been flirtatious before, but Gia thought she was being overly sensitive. She brought it up to her supervisor, and her supervisor said that Theo "talks like that to everyone" and "is from a different time." Gia got the impression that her supervisor thought she was overreacting, and she continued to meet with Theo alone. She was learning a lot from him, after all.

Last week, their meeting felt different. He asked if they could reschedule from lunch to evening. Gia's heart started pounding as she realized that the people working in administrative offices likely wouldn't be around in the evening—but she didn't want to offend Theo. She showed up for their meeting as usual.

Theo sexually assaulted Gia that night. Gia left his office feeling humiliated and terrified and blaming herself. Why didn't she listen to *her feelings that it wasn't safe to meet with Theo alone? Her mind was racing and she called Samantha and told her what happened.*

Samantha dropped everything she was doing and raced to Gia's side. Gia decided she wanted to contact a rape survivor advocacy group and take part in a rape kit exam. She doesn't know yet whether she would like to press charges or to report the assault to the administration at her hospital. She's taken an indefinite and unpaid leave from work.

Samantha notices that Gia has withdrawn not only from their relationship, but also from her life. She stays in their bedroom all day and doesn't want to see friends or engage in any of the activities they usually do together. Frequently, Samantha hears Gia crying, but when she goes to sit with her, Gia asks her to leave or walks away herself.

Samantha is angry. She is angry at Theo for assaulting Gia. She is angry at the hospital for being an unsafe work environment for Gia. She's angry at the officer they spoke to after the assault and how they treated Gia. She's angry at herself for not knowing how to support Gia. If she's really honest with herself, a part of her is even angry at Gia.

As for Gia, she doesn't know how she feels anymore; she feels nothing. She tries not to think about the assault, but every time she does, she plays over and over what she thinks she did wrong. She doesn't want to go back to work at the hospital; she doesn't know whether she'll ever feel safe to trust herself out in the world again.

As you read Gia and Samantha's story, do you identify with anything? Why do you think Samantha is so angry? Why do you think Gia blames herself? Do you think that's fair?

• Jennifer and Todd

Jennifer (she/her) and Todd (he/him) have been married for twenty-five years and have two adult children. They are about ten years out from retirement, but they're already enjoying their empty nest. They relish time together trying new restaurants, taking trips in the summer, and hanging out at home.

They are no strangers to the ups and downs in long-term love. They feel like they've navigated so much together: first jobs, buying a home, coping with in-law tension, raising children, that one year when Todd was out of work, and somehow figuring out how to pay for college for their kids.

Their friends think of them as a model couple. They rarely argue anymore, and they enjoy sex with each other on an almost weekly basis. Yes, they get on each other's nerves sometimes, but they are in it for the long haul and they love each other deeply.

Jennifer just watched a documentary on the #MeToo movement. It really got her *thinking. She keeps flashing back to different encounters that she had always written off as "boys will be boys." Her manager at the pizza parlor when she was a teen and how he would watch her and sometimes touch her in ways that felt uncomfortable. Her uncle, who commented on her developing breasts when she was only thirteen! Her first college boyfriend, who didn't much care for foreplay and wouldn't really tune in to her at all during sex ... was that even consensual?*

Jennifer's angry as she thinks about these encounters. Why wasn't she told these things weren't okay? Why didn't anyone teach these "boys" to respect women? Jennifer and Todd's daughters are young adults now—what if they didn't teach them everything they could to keep them safe?

Todd's confused. Some of these #MeToo stories sound like a big misunderstanding, and he tells this to Jennifer. Todd even considers himself a feminist, but he can't help but think some of these misunderstandings wouldn't have happened if the woman in the story could have just said no or not gotten herself into these situations. Yes, sometimes it's black and white, but so much of the time it seems like things could be resolved if women were just clearer about what they want or don't want. He thinks he might share this with his daughters.

When Todd tells this to Jennifer, Jennifer loses it. He just doesn't get it. Who is she even married to? She tells him he is victim blaming. That he's a typical man: mansplaining, dismissing, centering his own privilege. He's part of the problem, she says.

Now Todd's really confused. What? What language is Jennifer even speaking? It sounds like she's been brainwashed. Can't we all just get along and use common sense? he wants to tell her. Not all men are bad.

Jennifer responds by listing all the ways Todd contributes to rape culture and enabling perpetrators. Todd couldn't be more overwhelmed and defensive. Jennifer doesn't want to be near Todd. She certainly doesn't feel like opening up to him about her own experiences or being intimate with him.

As you read Jennifer and Todd's story, is there anything you can relate to? Why do you think Jennifer is so worked up? What does she want Todd to understand? Why is Todd so confused and what else might he be feeling? Is there anything Todd could have done differently in their interactions?

• Julia and Nico

Julia (she/her) met Nico (they/them) three months ago. It's rare for her to hit it off so well with a new person. On their first date, they stayed up for hours discussing their favorite movies and bands. About a week into their relationship, they figured out they used to go to the same summer camp. What are the chances?

Julia is nervous because she knows Nico would like to move forward in their sexual relationship. Julia has had sex before with a handful of partners, but she's always thought something was wrong with her sexually because of what happened in her childhood.

Julia's aunt molested and raped her on and off for many years in her childhood. Julia has never told anyone other than one therapist, whom she only had one session with a few years ago. It's really hard for her to talk about what happened with her aunt. In fact, it's easier to pretend it didn't happen at all even though it comes back to her sometimes in nightmares or flashbacks.

When Julia has had sex consensually in the past, she has kind of shut down during it. Her partners have told her that it seems like she's not that into it. The relationships haven't lasted very long. It's pretty confusing for her because she seems to have a pattern of falling hard for people, finding them very attractive, fantasizing about them while masturbating, and really looking forward to starting a sexual relationship. She's even the initiator a lot of the time.

But then, the sex itself never goes well. She wants to enjoy it, but once it starts getting more intimate, it's like she kind of checks out. Sometimes she feels irritable afterward and *starts picking fights. Sometimes, she is out of it for a few days and it's like she's in a fog.*

She hasn't shared any of this with Nico yet, but something is different about them. She thinks she wants to tell them about these experiences, but she isn't sure how to share or whether they'd even want to know.

As you read Julia and Nico's story, do you identify with anything they are experiencing? Do you think Julia should open up to Nico? Why or why not? Do you think Nico would want to know? How might they feel once they know her story and feelings? What did you think about these stories? Some of them may have been hard to read because of the feelings they brought up for you. Some may be similar to your and your partner's story, but some may be wildly different.

Did you notice any similarities between the stories? I did. In all of the stories, I felt a connection to how much these survivors and their partners care about each other. How much they both want to feel understood, want to feel connected. How lost and alone they feel in the wake of the impact of prior sexual trauma, no matter how long it's been since the trauma took place.

You might have identified with this. No matter how long ago your partner's trauma was, what is very real for you is that it's affecting you both right now. That's what trauma does. It brings the past into the present without warning and without permission. It sucks.

What I know deep in my heart, though, is that love and connection heal; love and connection offer hope. Your love and caring for your partner led you to this book. I bet you never thought you'd be reading a book like this, and yet here you are. You want to support your partner in their healing and you are open to doing some of your own work and research so that you can do it effectively. Isn't that amazing?

I'm going to let you in on a little secret. Trauma heals within safe, secure, and trusting relationships. If this is the type of relationship you and your partner have created (or are working to create), you are in one of the best positions to support your partner. This is true even if it feels like you've been getting everything wrong up until now or like you are eons away from understanding your partner.

You are here and that is a huge step.

The other side of the coin is that even though you might be one of your partner's best supports, you likely have gotten things wrong sometimes, and will absolutely continue to do so. That's okay. This book will help you better understand your partner and help you get it wrong less often. It will also help you feel more confident about how to handle the moments you might get it wrong—which, again, happen to all of us.

This chapter started with relatable stories, but now we will head into some information that might be new to you—the science of sexual trauma. You might have a lot of questions about sexual trauma as a phenomenon. How often is it really taking place? What even is it? What does it look like? Is my partner normal?

I'll tell you right now: yes, your partner is normal. Let's dive into some facts about what they're facing to help you better understand them.

What Is Sexual Trauma?

Sexual trauma, from a psychological point of view, is when a person experiences a sexual behavior inflicted upon them by another that causes intense fear and stress. We can experience a sexual trauma at any age, and we may or may not be fully aware of the trauma or impact on us immediately. Someone who's survived sexual trauma may have a diagnosis of acute stress disorder or posttraumatic stress disorder, or they may not. Either way, what they are experiencing may be confusing and overwhelming for their partner and may lead to emotional distress for both partners, including distress about the relationship. Additionally, survivors often find themselves triggered *within* the context of their intimate relationships—during sexual and physical intimacy, during anxiety-provoking emotional intimacy, or during conflict. As for their partners, they usually want guidance on how to support their partner as well as how to cope with the impact of their partner's past trauma on themselves.

As a partner of a sexual trauma survivor, you may feel confused, overwhelmed, and not sure how to support your partner. Within your relationship, you may feel frustrated, sad, helpless, disconnected, and unsure of how to deal with your anger toward your partner's perpetrator or the situation. You want to be close to your partner (again or for the first time), and you hope your partner can learn to relax within your relationship and be able to move on from their trauma.

Know that you're not alone with what you're facing and what you're feeling. And know that there are skills you can learn to help your partner feel understood, safe, and loved, and to keep the two of you connected and your relationship strong. It starts by understanding what your partner may have been through. So, we'll look at some common types of sexual trauma people can experience. Some of what you read here might be intense to contemplate. Pace yourself and take whatever time you need as you read.

Childhood Sexual Abuse and Molestation: Children are especially vulnerable to sexual abuse because they are dependent on adults for safety and protection. They are also too young to understand sexual boundaries and they cannot provide appropriate consent to sexual activity. Most people who abuse children sexually are close to or a member of the victim's family or a trusted person in the child's life. The abuser can groom children and their caregivers by giving gifts and attention, building trust, and manipulating the victim to believe they should not tell anyone about the abuse. Many children who experience sexual abuse internalize shame and guilt. They believe the abuse was their fault. Many survivors either keep the abuse a secret or, if they do come forward, experience further hurt when adults either don't believe them, don't do anything to protect them, or mishandle the information.

Incest: An incestual sexual relationship may be between a parent/grandparent/other adult family member and a child or between two related children or two related adults. Incest is especially traumatic for the survivor when one or both family members are children, dependents, or have been forced/manipulated into the sexual relationship. While all sexual abuse can bring up feelings of shame, the taboo experience of incest increases the likelihood that the survivor does not have a safe place to process their experience without judgment.

Emotional Sexual Abuse and Sexual Harassment: Emotional sexual abuse can look like sex shaming; controlling or manipulating a person in a sexual way;

discriminating against someone because of their gender, sex, or sexual identity; using sex or the withholding of sex to control someone; or unwelcome comments about another person's body. Most if not all physical sexual trauma includes emotional sexual abuse, but emotional sexual abuse might be present without a physical trauma.

Religious or Cultural Sexual Abuse: Sometimes cultural or religious practices around sex and sexuality can be traumatic for participants. This can include rigid gender/sex roles in relationships, rules and requirements around sex and sexuality that all persons involved in the religion or culture are expected to follow in order to remain a part of the community, rituals or practices that increase sexual shame or fear, forced sexual partnerships, forced changes or medical procedures to genitalia, and misinformation on sex and sexuality used to control or manipulate members of the community. Because these experiences and messages often come from people the survivor loves and trusts, the experience of religious or cultural sexual abuse can be particularly confusing and isolating for the survivor.

Sexual Assault: Some forms of sexual assault include attempted rape; fondling or unwanted sexual touching; forcing a victim to perform sexual acts, such as oral sex or penetration of the perpetrator's body; and penetration of the victim's body (also known as rape). It's important to note that force doesn't need to be physical; it may include coercion, emotional manipulation, psychological abuse, threats, and intimidation.

Date/Acquaintance Rape: This term describes rapes that are perpetrated by someone the survivor knows—as the majority of rapes are. This can be confusing for the survivor as they question their own decisions and perhaps even feel like the rape was their fault. The perpetrator may also continue a friendship or relationship with the survivor while using tactics to dismiss, deny, or blame as they hold true to their innocence.

Marital Rape: This is rape that occurs within a marriage. Just because a couple is married does not mean either partner can have sex with the other partner without their consent. This may be in conflict with a survivor's religious or cultural views and even the law. Marital rape is rarely spoken about, and someone who's survived it may never feel comfortable disclosing their experiences.

Military Sexual Trauma: Sexual assault and harassment is present in the military, and unfortunately the military has a poor history of protecting and believing the survivors. Survivors who experienced sexual trauma while serving may be scared to report for fear of consequences, alienation, or increased harassment by colleagues. Veterans often seek community with other veterans, but when a survivor's time in the military is marked by sexual trauma, a person may feel especially isolated because they might not feel comfortable continuing friendships with people who remind them of their trauma.

Corrective Rape: Corrective rape is a hate crime in which someone is raped because of their known or perceived sexual/gender orientation. The perpetrator may be intending to "turn" a person heterosexual or "force" them to present as cisgender (i.e., identifying as the gender they were assigned at birth).

As you can tell from these many types of assault, a key element that makes the experience of sexual assault so traumatic is the lack of *consent*. And so, a key intervention in helping your partner feel supported—one you can begin implementing right away—is letting them know that their consent to intimacy of any kind, including any discussion of their experience as a survivor, matters.

The Importance of Consent and How to Practice It

Consent, in the experience of intimacy, means that the people involved in a particular act or arrangement actively agree with what they are doing together. They make a decision together without manipulation by other parties (examples: coercion or force). A good standard is to only assume something is consensual if there has been verbal consent, such as saying "yes." I like to say that something is consensual when there is an "enthusiastic yes" or, in other words, no one is showing verbal or nonverbal signs that they are only saying yes out of fear.

Because lack of consent is so central to the experience of sexual trauma, practicing consent in a relationship is an important way to help your partner heal. This isn't only related to sexual intimacy—you may practice consent in regular day-to-day interactions or when discussing your partner's trauma.

Here are some ways you can practice consent:
- Have a conversation with your partner about consent and the ways you would each prefer to discuss, receive, and give consent. Revisit the conversation as needed.

- Reassure your partner that it is okay to say no to you at any point, whether you ask for consent or not.
- When you are in a sexual or romantic situation, ask your partner if they are comfortable. Examples: "Do you want to keep going?" "Is this okay?" "Are you comfortable?"
- When you've asked for consent or if something you'd like to do is okay, wait for a verbal communication from your partner, such as saying "yes." They may also give clear body language consent, such as nodding their head. If they are silent, say "no," don't seem to be enjoying themselves, or are resisting, know that you have not received consent.
- If your partner asks you for consent, always answer honestly and verbally. Thank them for having consent conversations with you.

Common Experiences and the Impact of Sexual Trauma

Now that you are more aware of just how common sexual trauma is, let's discuss the impact of sexual trauma on a survivor, including the possible ways that their emotional, mental, relational, and physical health are affected by sexual trauma. I hope that by reading more about these impacts, you will be able to feel some relief that what your partner has shared with you or what you have observed is normal. It's very important to survivors and the people who love them that their response to their trauma be accepted as normal because trauma can be a very isolating experience that can lead the survivor to feel ashamed of themself and how they are coping.

Loss of Trust

One of the hardest parts about experiencing trauma is that the experience may completely deteriorate the survivor's sense of trust and safety—in others, and in themselves.

Loss of Trust in Others

This may be the easiest aspect for those of us who haven't experienced sexual trauma to understand. It's not difficult to see how if someone hurts you very badly, you'll end up having a hard time trusting other people. And as you've learned, the majority of sexual violence is inflicted upon a survivor by someone they know or are close to. This can worsen the wound: learning that even someone you trust can hurt you can make relationships feel extremely risky.

When a survivor is hurt by someone they are close to, they can feel a lot of confusion. They may like or love this person. They may have felt very safe with this person. And then this person harmed them very badly. It's hard for the brain to make sense of this. A survivor in this position might play back other interactions with this person to try to find out what "went wrong." And a normal response may be to retreat from others because they don't know whether they are able to predict who is a safe person and who isn't.

Loss of Trust in Society and Their Environment

It's also common for a survivor to feel disillusioned by their environment or the society or communities of which they are a part. If their trauma was inflicted by a family member, for instance, how much can they trust their family? If their trauma happened in the workplace, how safe can they feel at work in the future? And this, too, makes sense, because they have painful evidence that their environment or community did not keep them safe.

Additionally, we are all constantly receiving messages that reinforce victim blaming. Your loved one hears these messages, too. What is victim blaming? *Victim blaming* is any statement that directly or indirectly suggests that the survivor is at fault for their assault or other sexual trauma.

Examples of victim blaming:
- A survivor tells a friend that their boyfriend had sex with them without their consent (rape), and the friend says, "Well, you wanted

to have sex with him anyway and it's not like you're a virgin—how was it?"
- A survivor reports sexual harassment at work to their supervisor, and the supervisor says, "Oh, I'm sure it's innocent fun—I know you love to joke around."
- A survivor reports their rape to a police officer, and the officer asks, "What were you wearing? Were you flirting with them?"
- A survivor tells a religious leader about abuse by someone in their religious community, and the leader reminds the survivor of the survivor's responsibility to practice abstinence until marriage and to not tempt others sexually.

Sexual assault and rape are dark parts of our culture. We don't want to believe it happens, and we really don't want to believe it can happen to us or someone we know or love. While it makes sense that we might look for other explanations when we're confronted by the reality of sexual violence, these types of statements are not helpful; they further reinforce the survivor's feelings that their environment and the people around them aren't safe.

Loss of Trust in Themselves

After surviving sexual trauma, it's common for survivors to feel that not only do they have a harder time trusting other people and the world around them, but they also have a hard time trusting themselves. Why is this?

Well, let's think back to the story of Gia and Samantha. Before she was assaulted, Gia had a generally hopeful and secure outlook on life. She was close to Samantha and her friends. She had strong professional relationships at work. She felt secure opening up to others and making connections to people in her various communities.

Theo, the person who assaulted her, was a mentor and her supervisor's boss. Gia had received reassurance from her supervisor that Theo was a safe person. What's more, Gia had participated in human resource trainings on sexual harassment and the zero-tolerance policy of sexual harassment or sexual relationships in the workplace, as is common in many workplaces. She had every reason to expect safety when meeting with Theo.

While Gia was nervous about some cues Theo was giving, women and other members of marginalized populations can experience anxiety about potential unsafe situations multiple times a day. Going out for a jog, walking their dog, walking to their car in a parking garage, sitting in their own living room and getting up multiple times to make sure the doors are locked, spending time with a friend of a friend who seems to intrude on physical boundaries, even going to a new coffee shop on a different side of town—women and other marginalized populations can already be incredibly vigilant and aware of their surroundings. And in order to get through life, many of us have learned to soothe our own anxieties so we can get on with our lives. While we may be nervous in any of the above situations, we still take part in those situations, and in life, with the hope and expectation that we will be safe. And this isn't an unfair expectation at all. All people have a right to safety. Ultimately, we all know Gia is not at fault for continuing to meet one-on-one with a professional mentor.

But after the sexual assault, Gia began questioning herself. Why hadn't she listened to the feeling she was having that something was off? Why didn't she insist on rescheduling to a time that she and Theo wouldn't be alone in the office? She may even go over what she was wearing and what signals she may have given off that made Theo think he could assault her or that sexual touch would be welcome. *Why did I trust that I'd be safe at work?* she might think. *Why did I trust Theo? Why did I trust myself?* And she might conclude with the thought: *I did so many things wrong.*

Again, Gia is in no way at fault for her assault. Even if Theo thought Gia was interested in a physical relationship, he did not seek consent. On top of that, the power dynamic between the two individuals—Theo's position of authority over Gia at their shared workplace—makes any sexual relationship questionable and unsafe for Gia. Finally, as the person holding the power in their relationship, it was Theo's explicit responsibility to not take advantage of Gia.

Even so, Gia and many survivors have a hard time quieting the voice in their head that is trying to understand why the assault happened and whether or how it could have been prevented. It is normal for a traumatized brain to think thoughts like *What did I do to cause this bad thing to happen?* or *Why didn't I make different decisions or act differently so this bad thing wouldn't have happened?*

Gia did not cause her assault. But her brain wants to help her make sure that something that bad doesn't happen again, so it's telling her she made a mistake and needs to learn from it to keep her safe. As she loses trust in herself, she retreats from the world, and her guilt and shame grow.

Retraumatization

Another common experience for sexual trauma survivors is the likelihood of retraumatization. What is retraumatization of a sexual trauma survivor? Imagine living through the scariest event or events of your life. You feel powerless, scared, violated, and betrayed. You are in physical and emotional pain because of the event(s). You feel isolated and alone. You need help. But every single time you ask someone for help, whether it's a friend, a family member, a doctor, a police officer, or even a therapist, they ask you to share what happened to you. You're already reliving the sexual trauma regularly in your mind during flashbacks or nightmares, but people are asking you to speak about your trauma. To describe what happened. And you feel pressured to do that so that you can get help—so that others know and understand why you need help. However, not only does it not seem to be getting you the help you need (because the emotional turmoil you are experiencing isn't going away), but it might actually be making it worse. Having to tell people about the most shameful and scary moments of your life—while you watch their faces judging you and they say a lot of wrong things—makes you feel even more alone. And you feel violated all over again. That's retraumatization.

There are many times a survivor may feel retraumatized; here are some:
- when they have to give multiple statements to officers (if they decide to involve law enforcement)
- when they're questioned or collectively shamed by others or the media if their story is shared publicly
- when reporting the sexual trauma to leaders in their school, workplace, place of worship, or other communities

- when they have to disclose the trauma to doctors, nurses, or other health professionals
- when looking for a therapist and having to repeatedly disclose their trauma
- when setting new or different emotional or physical boundaries with others and experiencing those boundaries as violated or disrespected
- when having an experience that triggers their trauma, and then being dismissed or judged by others
- when telling a friend, partner, or family member, and that person, despite possibly having good intentions, does any of the following:
  - asks too many questions about details
  - looks for other explanations
  - tells them what they should do and gives unsolicited advice
  - doesn't say anything at all
  - victim blames

Regardless of the way a survivor experiences retraumatization, it may exacerbate any of the emotions or symptoms they have been experiencing and may increase the chance that the survivor experiences posttraumatic stress disorder.

Posttraumatic Stress Disorder and Symptoms

The majority of survivors of sexual trauma will experience symptoms of posttraumatic stress disorder (PTSD) or acute stress disorder. While the survivor in your life may not meet all the criteria for either of these mental health diagnoses, it can be helpful to understand the symptoms of these disorders that are recognized in the mental health community.

At the time of writing this book, the *Diagnostic and Statistical Manual of Mental Disorders* (edition 5-TR; American Psychiatric Association 2022) is the most recent edition of the manual referred to by medical and mental health providers to diagnose mental health symptomology.

Some symptoms of PTSD include:
1. Reexperiencing the traumatic event through flashbacks, intrusive thoughts, or nightmares.
2. Avoiding situations, places, people, thoughts, and feelings that remind one of the traumatic event.
3. Negative beliefs, thoughts, and feelings that are associated with the trauma and/or became worse after the traumatic event.
4. Reactive moods and feelings, hypervigilance, and/or outbursts.

5. Dissociative symptoms, including depersonalization (feeling out of body, detached, or dreamlike) or derealization (the world feels unreal, detached from reality).

These symptoms can occur at any time following the traumatic event (if the onset is beyond six months after the traumatic event, it is considered "delayed onset") and can last for any length of time. In acute stress disorder, the same symptoms are present, but the duration is shorter, lasting from three days to one month following the traumatic event.

What was it like to consider this list of symptoms? Did you see any that your partner seems to experience? You may recognize many of these symptoms in your partner, or you may not recognize any at all. Ultimately, your partner is the expert on their own experience and the best person to identify these symptoms in themselves, so always ask permission to discuss these symptoms or diagnosis with your partner, as they may not want or be ready to explore a diagnosis. Also, while it can be helpful to use diagnosis language to understand your partner's experience, help their symptoms make sense, and help a mental health professional support your partner, your partner may perceive a diagnosis negatively, and that is valid. Your partner's life and experience is unique, and attaching a label to their emotional response can feel invalidating to some. Tread lightly here to remain supportive of your partner.

Relational Impact

We talked earlier about the potential impact on a survivor's ability to trust others. They may lean out of relationships, including friendships, to avoid situations where they could be hurt by someone again, or they may lean in to relationships for reassurance. I like to frame these reactions as normal and through the lens of attachment science—the science of how we learn to relate to others based on the ways our caregivers did or didn't take care of us when we were young. Attachment plays a major role in our relationships, so let's dive into this a bit.

Attachment Theory

John Bowlby and Mary Ainsworth were the first psychologists to study and observe attachment in child–caregiver relationships. Children are born into the world ready and desiring to attach securely to the person who is keeping them safe. In order for children to feel safe, they need food, shelter, comfort, and attention (Bowlby et al. 1956). While this may seem obvious to us in this day and age, it wasn't until Bowlby and Ainsworth studied child–parent relationships more closely that we really understood comfort, love, and attention as basic human needs for healthy development.

We now also understand that these emotional experiences are needed in adult relationships and not only when we are developing as children. If we feel emotionally safe, understood, and supported in a primary relationship as adults, we feel more secure in all areas of our life. Love isn't only romantic fluff; it is a basic need. What's more, how attuned our parents or caregivers were to us growing up, and how safe and connected we've felt in our important primary relationships, largely determines how we'll show up in our life and in relationships. How we relate to those who matter most to us is what's known as our *attachment style*.

Attachment styles are on a spectrum, and at different times in our lives we may relate more to different styles. Our attachment styles are also malleable; we can feel more secure in our relationships if we had significant positive experiences in primary relationships, we can feel less secure if we had significant negative experiences, and we can build our sense of relational security in our relationships going forward even if past experiences have made our attachment styles less secure. Still, it'll be helpful to get a sense of your partner's and your own general attachment style at this moment in time so you have a place to start building a more secure relationship for the both of you.

Scientists who study attachment have boiled attachment styles down to four broad categories: secure attachment, avoidant attachment, anxious attachment, and disorganized attachment. Let's take a look at each of them now, and see whether we can get a sense of where you and your partner might be falling most often.

Secure Attachment

Ideally, when we communicate to someone we love that we need their support, they will respond to us consistently. If we have a bad day, they are there to talk about it. When we are ill, they check in and support us. When we are sad, they reach out to us with comfort. When this type of consistent emotional support is provided in a relationship, we feel secure. We know our partner is there for us. We trust the relationship, and we feel good when we are together and good when we are apart. Even when we face hard things (in the relationship or outside of it), we know our relationship is a safe place that we can seek support and explore ways to cope.

Someone who has a secure attachment style, either because they bonded to their caregiver securely in childhood or they experienced securely attached adult relationships, has strong self-worth and desires close relationships.

A survivor of sexual trauma may have a secure attachment style, despite their past trauma, as a result of attuned early caregivers and safe and comforting relationships in the present.

Avoidant Attachment

Someone with an avoidant attachment style may appear emotionally unavailable or unaware of their partner's emotional needs. You may be in distress and communicating this, but your partner with an avoidant attachment style does not respond. If they do respond, they may encourage you to be stronger and less emotional. Your partner might also particularly value their own independence and tend not to ask for support from others, including you.

People with an avoidant attachment style may have been emotionally neglected and dismissed by their primary caregiver. Or, they may have had long-term relationships with people with an avoidant attachment style and coped by detaching from emotions and closeness themselves. In this way, their avoidant attachment style is a way to cope with the pain of not being supported in times of need by people they love. By distancing themselves from people they love, a person with an avoidant style manages to avoid the experiences of being rejected or ignored.

Survivors of sexual trauma may develop an avoidant attachment style as a response to the trauma they've been through and the experience of being betrayed or let down by people they know or just people in general.

Anxious Attachment

When someone has experienced inconsistent support from a caregiver or an adult with whom they were in a close relationship, they may have an anxious attachment style—which can also be known as an ambivalent or a preoccupied attachment style. People with this type of attachment style often feel confused and insecure in relationships. They seek closeness and may even be judged as clingy, but at the same time they may feel suspicious or untrusting of their partner. If your partner has this attachment style, they may check in with you frequently, seek constant reassurance (without relief), and doubt how much you care about them. They may fixate or obsess on details or times they've felt hurt in the relationship.

Survivors of sexual trauma may develop an anxious attachment style as a response to the trauma they've been through and the experience of having inconsistent support or predictability in either the relationship with their perpetrator or those they turn to for support.

Disorganized Attachment

Someone who has experienced physical or emotional abuse, cruelty, or terrifying behavior may develop a disorganized, also known as fearful-avoidant, attachment style. When experiencing abuse, a person may dissociate from themselves and/or their surroundings in order to cope. They have to detach from what is happening to them in order to survive the immense distress they are experiencing.

A survivor of sexual trauma may develop a disorganized attachment style as a response to their trauma. A partner with this attachment style may seem detached from themselves and others. They may enjoy relationships but become uncomfortable after a certain amount of intimacy that feels "too close" emotionally. Being close feels unsafe because of their past abuse; they relive their trauma when experiencing a certain level of intimacy. They may seem unpredictable in a relationship, both pushing their partner away and pulling them closer.

What's your sense of your partner's attachment style? What's your sense of your own? How do you feel the two are meshing, or not meshing, at this point in time? This is important for you to understand because some of the ways you are experiencing your partner's behavior may seem confusing to you but actually make a lot of sense because of how their attachment has been impacted by their trauma.

Below is a list of behaviors that can signal that trauma has affected a person's ability to relate and connect to those they love. See how many match your experience with your partner.

- Not wanting to be alone and needing extra comfort and reassurance
- Getting overwhelmed easily during conflict
- Getting overwhelmed easily during emotional or physical intimacy
- Quickly becoming irritable or critical of you
- Seeming angry at you
- Pulling away and not allowing any emotional or physical closeness
- Pushing you away when you try to help
- Seeming like they are giving up on you and your relationship
- Seeking extra attention from you or others
- Detaching from the world or others
- Shutting down and avoiding conversation

If you've experienced any of these behaviors from your partner, it can be dispiriting, even heartbreaking. But when you consider how the sexual trauma your partner experienced may have impacted their sense of security in close relationships, it might be easier to understand.

What is really amazing in attachment theory is that building or rebuilding trust and safety within a primary relationship is the best way for someone to move toward a more secure feeling—not only within the relationship, but also in their life.

This is a role you may be able to play for your partner and this is why I'm writing this book: to help loving partners like you know how to build that sense of security with and for your partner so that you can help their healing, while also creating or moving back toward a loving, nurturing, and reciprocal relationship.

With that, let's look at some of the emotional experiences that are common among survivors of sexual trauma so you can learn to respond in ways that promote healing.

Common Emotional Experiences of Survivors of Sexual Trauma

It is normal to be overwhelmed by the intense emotions your partner is experiencing. You might see them in pain and want desperately to help them out of it but have no idea how. You might be worried about whether they are in danger of falling so deeply into their "negative" emotions that they will experience too much emotional suffering, get "stuck in negativity," or face other painful consequences or losses.

This makes sense because you care deeply about your partner, and when we care about someone who's in deep pain, particularly when that pain is not their fault, we sometimes have the urge to help them "fix" the negative emotions. But what will likely be more helpful to your partner's well-being and mental health is showing them that you are strong enough to see and accept their emotions as a normal reaction to the trauma they experienced.

Survivors are often better able to get through the emotional roller coaster they are on if they are met with empathy and validation of their feelings, and if those feelings are normalized as understandable human responses to trauma, rather than stigmatized as something that can and should "just go away."

Chapter 4, on communication, will go more deeply into how you can communicate this empathy, validation, and normalization. In the meantime, let's work on building that empathy. I would like to give you a picture of the many emotions you may be observing in your partner so you can understand why these emotions come up and why they are actually helpful to the healing process.

Anger

Anger is a very helpful emotion. The need for safety is both physical and emotional, and in the moments we feel unsafe, anger protects us by signaling that we do not feel safe and need a change.

A sexual trauma survivor has had their sense of safety violated, and their body and mind are working to help them re-establish safety and security. At the same time, many cultures give direct or indirect messages that anger is not an acceptable emotion to feel or express. And you may have your own conflicted thoughts and feelings about anger. This might make it hard for you to support your partner when they are angry because their anger may trigger a threat to your own sense of safety.

Try to connect with the idea that anger can actually empower your partner in their healing—if it's felt and expressed in healthy ways and met with understanding and kindness. When your partner is able to feel and express their anger, they may be better able to move away from the feelings of guilt and shame that can be especially debilitating.

Of course, anger can also be internalized, or it may be impossible to direct it at its true target, so your partner may feel angry with themself and even with you. This may be frustrating for you, especially when you feel the only person they should be angry with is the perpetrator of the trauma. This is likely confusing to your partner as well, and they may swim around in the experience of anger for a while before it is processed in a way that is most helpful to their healing.

Fear and Terror

Fear and terror might be the emotions that make the most sense to you. When someone has a sexual traumatic experience, the emotions of fear and terror may be so overwhelming in the moment that they disconnect from themselves and their surroundings. And the trauma can then keep the emotional experience of fear present, or very easily triggered, when it seems unwarranted.

When we see our partner in fear, it can be instinctual to tell them that there is nothing to be scared about. And that might feel very true to us in that moment, but it can also end up being dismissive of their feelings. In times like these, it can help to remember that your partner cannot help but feel the fear that is triggered in that moment—and that fear may feel as strong as it felt during the initial trauma. What may be more helpful when they are scared is letting them know that it makes sense that they feel this way and that you're there for them. We will discuss more ways you can support a partner when they are triggered later in the book.

Sadness and Grief

Sadness and grief can show up for many different reasons when someone is healing from sexual trauma. Because sadness can be quite a vulnerable feeling, and a survivor likely has been betrayed, violated, and hurt in many ways, the sadness may be buried underneath their other emotions. It might only come out with people they trust, like you, a close friend or family member, or a therapist. It might not come up at all.

Alternatively, it may feel like sadness is all your partner feels. It may seem overwhelming, and you might be worried that they will not get past the sadness and be able to enjoy the good things in life again.

There is nothing wrong with sadness; sadness is a very helpful if painful emotion. Sadness is our way of cuing to ourselves and others that we are hurting and need support. The best thing you can do for someone who is sad is to not pressure them to move on and to let them know they are not alone, that their sadness will not cause you to reject them or abandon them. You can show them this in your words and actions.

Shock, Numbness, and Avoidance

At times it might seem like your partner is numb. They simply say they feel "fine" or they feel "nothing," even when it's clear to you that they're going through something. This is especially common soon after a trauma or after retraumatization. The pain of the experience they've had can be so great that they go numb to protect themself. Your partner's not lying to you in such moments; they may truly feel numb inside because their body is protecting them from the overwhelming pain of their experience. Know that that shock and numbness is a healthy way of coping with trauma, especially in the early stages, and try not to pressure your partner to talk about things or to feel a certain way. Instead, be as open as you can to what they feel and try to meet them where they are, letting them know, again, that you're there for them and you care about them deeply.

If it seems like your partner is using substances, food, television, work, or other behaviors to distract themself and avoid their feelings, please know that this is also a common way of coping. And while some distraction and avoidance is helpful, some can be destructive and cause more pain. In these cases, it's okay to let your partner know you are worried about them and that you would like to help them get help. Use a gentle, nonjudgmental, and nonconfrontational tone. We will discuss this in more detail later in the book.

Putting It All Together

This chapter focused on sharing the realities and common experiences of survivors of sexual trauma. You may already have known a lot of the information shared in this chapter, or maybe a lot of it is new to you. The survivor stories may have left you feeling sad, mad, hopeless, or all three—those are normal feelings to have when we sit in compassion and empathy for people who have survived violence at the hands of another person. This brings us to what we'll focus on in the next chapter: the impact of sexual trauma on you and your relationship. Your feelings about your partner's trauma may feel like a roller coaster and the impact of the trauma on your relationship may be quite confusing. Let's work to understand these experiences together in chapter 2.

CHAPTER 2

Impact of Sexual Trauma on Your Relationship

In the last chapter, we reviewed the many ways that sexual trauma may be impacting your partner. I hope that after reading through example stories, types of sexual trauma that people can experience, and descriptions of common emotional experiences of survivors, you are coming into this chapter with a better understanding of your partner and the ways they may be feeling and acting.

This chapter will look more closely at the many different ways you might be feeling and coping as your partner's sexual trauma impacts you and your relationship. Your partner is important to you, and you may see them in pain, confusion, and fear when they are triggered or processing their experience. Seeing someone we love experience or heal from a traumatic event can be very distressing. You may want to support them but not know what to do or say. You may be scared, angry, or panicked yourself. On top of these very understandable feelings, your partner likely isn't in a place to be a support to you because they are the one who lived through the trauma. Finally, you might not know whether what you are experiencing is normal and you might not know to whom to turn.

I'm so glad you sought out this book so that you don't have to go through this challenging time alone. I hope this chapter normalizes what you've been going through, helps you put words to what you are feeling, and begins to give you some new ways to cope. In this chapter, we'll work to help identify how you've been feeling and coping, explore how the trauma has impacted your relationship, and begin to see different ways you and your partner can connect while healing from the sexual trauma they've experienced.

Your journey as a partner of a sexual trauma survivor hasn't been easy so far, and there isn't an easy path to calm and reconnection. But what I do know from working for years with sexual trauma survivors and their partners is that you two are capable of tremendous healing and closeness as you walk this path together.

Setting the Stage

In just a moment we're going to dive into the stories of couples we read about in chapter 1. Before we do this, you might take a moment to journal or reflect on the following questions. Answers may or may not come easily. Either is okay. As you start to find the words for your own story, you are getting closer to being able to process and move through your own emotional trauma of this experience.

1. How have you been feeling since you found out about your partner's sexual trauma?
2. Have you noticed yourself thinking about it a lot? If so, what is that like?
3. Are you often caught off guard by your partner's reactions? If so, what is that like?
4. Do you have anyone to turn to during this time or have you been feeling alone with the impact?
5. What have you been doing to take care of yourself? Of your partner? How has that been helping (or not helping)?

Reflecting on this experience may be distressing. If you become overwhelmed or distressed while reading this book, now or at any point, please know that that can be a normal response. It's okay to take breaks from the book and your journaling or reflecting. You might take time to soothe yourself with music, a walk outside, or a relaxing shower. We'll also work to identify additional soothing activities you can practice in chapter 3.

It's also crucial to remember that you're not alone in your experience, no matter how much it might feel like it sometimes. Let's return to the couples you met in the previous chapter to see how they too struggle with the impact of their partner's experience of sexual trauma on their relationships. After reading each description, you'll find questions to reflect on. If you feel inclined, you can write your responses to these questions in your journal.

• *Thomas and Marina*

Thomas has been thinking more about what Marina shared about feeling pressured each time he asks her to spend time with him or he tries to get close to her physically, and about how he is triggering her memories of her emotionally and sexually abusive ex-boyfriend.

Thomas just doesn't understand why she's feeling this way. He's never been abusive to her; he loves her and wants to protect her. It's especially confusing because she used to seem so relaxed whenever they spent time together—how can she see him as the cause of stress now?

It feels to Thomas like he's walking on eggshells with Marina. Every time he brings up the matter of their intimacy, or makes a move, she seems so angry with him. She's told him that she does want things to get better with him but that it seems like he only initiates things with her when she's overwhelmed or exhausted. And with an infant, when is she not feeling overwhelmed and exhausted?

What's more, Thomas knows that when he's stressed, spending time with Marina connecting emotionally and sexually is the best way to help him feel better. Shouldn't it be the same for her? And he's worried that if they don't do something about the distance growing between them now, they will never return to that feeling of closeness and security that he misses so much.

He tries everything. He asks her to go to therapy, he prints out tips for having sex after becoming parents and gives them to her, and he buys her lingerie and gifts. Yet it seems like she's pulling more and more away. They start to bicker more and Thomas is getting pretty worried that things won't get better.

REFLECTION QUESTIONS

How is Thomas feeling and why? Have you felt this way?

Thomas seems to be coping by pointing Marina to resources and giving her gifts, but this doesn't seem to be helping the situation. Based on what Marina has shared (that it's hard when she feels pressured), how do you think this affects Marina?

What does Thomas want Marina to understand? What might Marina need from Thomas?

- *Favor and Frank*

After Frank told Favor about the rape he experienced, both partners have been careful with each other. Frank still feels embarrassed *that he had a flashback while in bed with Favor. He doesn't want Favor to think he's fragile or broken. He's thinking about the interaction a lot but hasn't brought it up again.*

Favor hasn't brought it up again either, and he's very nervous about triggering Frank again. He loves Frank and it was painful to see him hurting so much. He wants to be a safe and loving space for Frank, not someone who triggers such a painful response.

Lately, things have been feeling a bit awkward in the relationship for both Favor and Frank. Sometimes it feels like it used to feel between them and Favor feels a desire to lean in for a kiss or playfully grab Frank's butt like he used to, but he stops himself for fear of triggering Frank again. Frank can tell this is happening, and it's just a reminder that there's something wrong with him. This is why he never wanted to tell Favor about the rape in the first place.

Even though Frank and Favor have had such a loving relationship, they've never had to talk about very serious things with each other. Neither of them came from families that talked a lot about feelings or vulnerable things, so it's hard to start doing it now with each other. It seems like they just don't have the words.

Favor wants to check in with Frank. He wants to know what Frank needs in order to not get triggered again. He wants both of them to find a way back to each other. Frank wants to reconnect with Favor, too. He wants to tell him that it's okay to get close. That he doesn't want his trauma to get in the way of their relationship. Both partners are struggling to communicate, so they go on avoiding talking about it and even avoiding pleasurable experiences with each other that could trigger the topic. Sex and intimacy remain the elephant in the room.

REFLECTION QUESTIONS

How is Favor feeling and why? Have you felt this way?

Favor seems to be coping by avoiding topics and situations that might trigger Frank. Based on how Frank is feeling inside, do you think this is helping the situation? Why or why not?

What is Favor afraid of? What is Frank afraid of?

• Gia and Samantha

When we last left Gia and Samantha, Gia was falling deeper into a depression and Samantha wasn't sure what to do to help her.

Samantha is still feeling angry. Gia has decided not to press charges, and Samantha can't believe she's not going to do anything. How can Theo just get away with ruining Gia's life? Ruining their lives? Theo is going on in his successful career, left to perpetrate again and again while Gia can't even leave her room? It isn't fair!

Gia said she isn't ready to start therapy, but Samantha is worried about this. She knows that survivors of sexual assault can fall into a deep depression and even become suicidal. She's tried to discuss this with Gia, but Gia seems to check out whenever she brings it up.

Samantha decided to start therapy on her own. She's starting to understand that the reason she feels so angry and irritable all the time is because she feels helpless in this situation. Like there's nothing she can do to make things better. She breaks down and cries in one session; she just feels so alone.

She thinks maybe she will ask Gia to come to an appointment with her or start couples therapy. She doesn't know whether Gia will agree, and she doesn't want to pressure her.

Samantha fantasizes about getting revenge on Theo sometimes. She wants to storm into that building and tell him off. Or make a report to HR on behalf of Gia. Or send a letter to Theo's wife and tell him what kind of man she's married to.

Gia agrees to come to a couples therapy session with Samantha, and Samantha shares these fantasies with Gia. Gia starts shaking and says Samantha's fantasies scare her. Samantha feels bad. She wouldn't really do any of the things in her fantasies, but she didn't want to make Gia feel worse. Gia says she isn't sure she wants to come to another session.

> ## REFLECTION QUESTIONS
>
> How is Samantha feeling and why? Have you felt this way?
>
> Samantha seems to be coping by feeling anger toward Theo, Gia's perpetrator, and wishing she could do something to punish him. Based on how Gia reacts to Samantha in their therapy session, do you think this is helping the situation? Why or why not?
>
> What is Samantha afraid of? What is Gia afraid of?

• Jennifer and Todd

After their big blow-up argument, Jennifer and Todd both took time to think about what their partner shared with them.

Jennifer is still annoyed about many of Todd's statements, but she loves Todd and decides she wants to help him better understand why she responded the way she did and how he is contributing to rape culture with some of his beliefs.

Initially Todd rolls his eyes and doesn't take the time to read the articles that Jennifer forwarded to him. But then he lowers his guard a bit and reads a personal account of someone *who was harassed at the workplace. What really got him was how long the workplace harassment stayed with the survivor; she only stayed at that job another year, but she felt insecure in future work settings, and it definitely took a toll on her mental health and confidence. He agreed that this wasn't right.*

He accepted Jennifer's invitation to watch a documentary on the topic of sexual harassment and assault. He started to understand his own privilege and how that kept him blind to so many issues that impact women and LGBTQ+ people in their day-to-day life. He asked Jennifer to share some of her experiences, and he became tearful as he thought about the ways she was objectified and disrespected throughout her life. Part of him wanted to ask his daughters about their experiences, too, but he was scared to know.

Todd began thinking about things he had done in the past. He's never raped anyone or exposed himself in the workplace—he's not a sicko. He has laughed along with the guys when they've told stories before, though. And there was that girlfriend in college who was nervous about having sex for the first time, and he wasn't exactly patient with her. It's becoming clearer to him that he's been part of the problem, too.

He's ashamed—and he doesn't know what to do with this guilt and shame. He thinks about calling up his college girlfriend and asking for forgiveness. He feels awkward around his friends, and even starts seeing some of them differently—the way they talk about women or treat their partners. He catches himself saying or thinking insensitive things sometimes; he finds himself overthinking things and not wanting to offend any of the women in his life (his wife, his daughters, his coworkers—so many people he could hurt or disrespect)!

He wants to get it right and doesn't want to contribute to a culture that degrades, objectifies, and traumatizes women.

> ## REFLECTION QUESTIONS
>
> How is Todd feeling and why? Have you felt this way?
>
> Originally Todd seemed to cope by dismissing and minimizing what Jennifer talked with him about. Why do you think he did this? Why might his reaction not be helpful and what might he do instead?
>
> Todd now seems to be coping by focusing on how he's contributed to rape culture. Do you think this is a helpful response?

• Julia and Nico

When we last left Julia and Nico, Julia was thinking about telling Nico about the ongoing molestation she experienced as a child and how *she thinks it affects her ability to stay present and connected during sex.*

Nico has noticed that Julia seems distracted or not all there during sex. They think maybe she's not that into them. It's confusing, because they get along so well and Julia seems into them when they joke around and start foreplay. Maybe they're not meeting her needs sexually. They start to feel insecure.

Julia can tell Nico is pulling away. She doesn't want to ruin this relationship and she trusts Nico. She tells them about the sexual abuse she experienced. She's scared as she talks about it with them, but Nico is comforting and reassures her that what happened wasn't her fault. At the end of the conversation, she feels a little embarrassed, but she's also relieved that she finally told someone she cares about. It brings them closer together emotionally.

It doesn't change their sex life, though. It still seems to Nico like Julia checks out during sex, and Nico still can't help but think that it's because they aren't a good enough lover. They feel themself pulling away sexually from her.

Julia sits down with Nico one day and shares that she just read about something called dissociation. She thinks maybe that's what's happening for her during sex. Dissociation is a way that trauma survivors cope with really overwhelming situations. That way she checks out? It probably started when she was a kid to protect herself during the abuse, she says.

Julia asks Nico whether they would come with her to see a sex therapist to help them find ways to connect without Julia dissociating. Nico wants to support Julia, but they haven't gone to therapy before and this all seems really overwhelming. They aren't sure whether it will help. And they're worried the therapist will tell them it's their fault, or Julia will tell them it's actually because she isn't attracted to them.

REFLECTION QUESTIONS

How is Nico feeling and why? Have you felt this way?

Nico seems to be coping by worrying that Julia's trauma symptoms are actually related to them not being a "good enough" partner or lover. Based on what Julia has shared with them, do you think this is helping the situation? Why or why not?

What is Nico afraid of? What is Julia afraid of?

As you read through these stories, you might have related to some of the reactions you saw; others, you might not relate to at all. Know that each of our experiences is unique, and your experience and ways of coping are unique to you. Also, when it comes to trauma, there isn't a "right way" to feel. Your feelings make sense no matter how confusing this might all be for you. I have a lot of compassion for the individuals depicted in the stories above, and I have a lot of compassion for you, too.

I've also noticed time and time again that when the work of healing gets tough, my clients find comfort in connecting with the strengths of their relationship and their positive intentions for the relationship. So, in the next section, we will explore the goals you have for your own trauma healing (because sexual trauma has a ripple effect around the survivor, which can traumatize loved ones) and the future of your relationship. We will use these intentions that you have for your relationship to lean on when it gets hard to keep working on your healing.

Setting an Intention for Your Healing

In this section, we will discuss why setting an intention is helpful and how you and your partner can use this resource as you work together to strengthen your relationship as your partner heals from their sexual trauma. Before we take the time to reflect on your goals and intentions for relationship healing, I'll offer a little pep talk that you may find yourself returning to when things feel stuck.

There is no clear time line we can expect when supporting our partners with their sexual trauma healing and strengthening our relationship. We also don't know exactly what the "end goal" is when we work on healing, because each survivor finds that their healing looks unique to them and their experience.

What we can work toward, though, is building a secure relationship. A secure relationship isn't a perfect-conflict-free-everyone's-happy-all-the-time relationship. A secure relationship is one where we and our partners move together in connection during times of distress; where each partner feels secure in themself as an individual and within the relationship; where each partner trusts that they can turn to each other when they need support—and when things don't go well within a relationship, they can trust that their partner will be there to help repair hurt feelings within the relationship.

Because there is no set time line for the work you'll do to heal, remind yourself to celebrate small victories. When you find yourself stuck in a moment of disconnection and both say hurtful things or become overwhelmed and run away from the pain, know that this doesn't invalidate the work you've already done on this relationship, and it isn't a sign that your relationship is hopeless. All relationships have conflict. Instead, celebrate the times that you are able to come back to each other and reconnect, each partner owning their own role in the conflict and working together to make things better.

With this note of encouragement to celebrate each small victory, let's use a journal exercise to set a clear intention for hope and healing for both you and your partner and the impact the sexual trauma has had on your relationship.

EXERCISE: Setting an Intention

For many activities in this book, you may choose to reflect in your mind or to journal your reflections. For this exercise in particular, it is especially helpful to write out your answers to the following prompts so that you have a tangible document you can return to in the future when things feel hard.

If your partner is open to participating in this exercise with you, it works well as a shared experience. It's okay to do this exercise independently if they are not able to participate, though, because your answers will still serve as support and motivation to you in the future.

- Reflect on the strengths of your relationship. What has drawn you together and keeps you both going in the relationship? If you were telling someone else everything you love about your relationship, what would you say?
- What strengths do you bring to your relationship? What strengths do you have

as an individual? How do these strengths support your partner and your relationship?

What strengths does your partner bring to your relationship? What strengths do they have as an individual? How do these strengths support you and your relationship?

What values do you share in your relationship that give meaning to your lives together? Examples of this are having similar beliefs, enjoying similar activities, or having similar dreams about your future together.

What, as best you can say, is your shared vision for the relationship as you both work to heal from the shared impact of the sexual trauma? What do you want to remember when things get hard in your relationship to keep you both going and moving forward?

Reflecting on the strengths of your relationship, the strengths each of you bring to it, and your shared values tends to serve as a reminder for why you want to do the work to support your partner. Now that you have an idea of what is motivating you to work on this and what you envision for your future in the relationship, we will spend some time discussing common emotional and coping experiences that you may relate to as a partner of a sexual trauma survivor.

How Are You Coping?

In chapter 1, we spent time learning about the different responses survivors of trauma can have, and how they're all normal. Because trauma impacts both the survivor and their loved ones, I hope it is a relief to you to know that it's also normal for you to be on your own emotional roller coaster. You may recognize some of the emotions and ways of coping we'll go on to discuss from the stories you read above, or from your own relationship. On the other hand, you might find that you don't relate much at all. That is okay! There is no right way to feel when we are seeing our loved one in pain. Above all, as I describe the different ways of feeling and coping below, be compassionate with yourself and whatever you might experience.

In the sections that follow, we'll look at particular ways you might be coping—feelings you might be having, ways you might be trying to help the situation, underlying emotional needs you might have, and the possible impact you might notice in your relationship.

Shutting Down or Avoiding the Topic

One way we cope as humans when we are overwhelmed is by shutting down or avoiding uncomfortable topics. This makes sense because as we are overwhelmed, we can become flooded with confusing emotions and feel like we need space so that we can feel calm again. Our bodies often give us physical cues when we are overwhelmed, such as our heart racing or our mind racing or going blank. But it might be hard to even know exactly how we are feeling when we are overwhelmed because we might be feeling lots of uncomfortable emotions at once: fear, panic, anger, sadness.

When this happens, you might notice that you shut down. Maybe your partner becomes triggered and you're so afraid of saying or doing the wrong thing that you go blank or get quiet. Maybe you feel so uncomfortable seeing the sadness and fear that your partner feels that you avoid the topic of the sexual assault or anything else that might trigger them because you don't want to hurt them. When you're doing this, you're not just trying to take care of yourself by focusing on more comfortable topics or trying to keep yourself calm; you're also trying to protect your partner from their pain. Shutting down, emotionally or behaviorally, might be the only thing we know how to do when facing a traumatic experience or highly emotionally charged topics.

If you notice yourself shutting down or avoiding uncomfortable topics and conversations with your partner, be kind to yourself. You are coping with a lot of stress and are looking for calm and a sense of safety for you and your partner. That makes sense!

Your partner might shut down as well when they're overwhelmed, or they might get frustrated or sad when it seems like you are shutting down, or they might become worried that you don't care. They may feel abandoned or rejected as they seek connection to you and encounter a shutdown response—not understanding the stress and fear you're feeling. Perhaps they can express this kindly in words you can understand—but they might also get triggered in the moment and become frustrated or upset with you for going quiet. This is because they are scared that they've lost connection with you, and that connection to you is one of the ways they try to bring themselves back to calm. Unfortunately, you might become even more overwhelmed when they become upset and feel yourself shutting down even more. Oh no! You've found yourself in a painful cycle where neither you nor your partner feels very connected or calm.

REFLECTION QUESTIONS

Does this pattern sound familiar to you?

How do you feel inside before or during your shutdown?

What are you afraid will happen if you talk about the trauma or respond to your partner when they are triggered?

Has anything been helpful when you have found yourselves in this pattern?

> *What would it be like to tell your partner about what you are feeling on the inside when it seems like you are shutting down?*
>
> *How do you think your partner feels on the inside when they notice you shutting down in this way?*

Wondering When Your Partner Will Feel Better

It is normal to want your partner to feel better and heal from their trauma. Of course you want them to be free of the pain they are experiencing because you love them and you have seen them struggling. Sometimes we become worried that our partner doesn't seem to be feeling better soon enough; it might feel like a lot of time has passed since the trauma, that they are in too much pain to get through the day, or that maybe they haven't done enough to get to a better place.

When you feel this way, you might start saying or doing things to nudge your partner in the direction of healing. Inside you might feel scared that they'll never feel better or "normal" again, or that you'll never be able to bond in the relationship without the risk of triggering them somehow. You might also feel helpless in the situation because you can't heal your partner or fix the situation as you might want to. And it's normal to start getting panicked when we feel helpless—no one likes feeling powerless in a situation! So, you might start saying things like "Do you think your therapy is helping you?" "Do you think it's normal to still get triggered by my touch after so many years?" "You know, I read an article on EMDR (eye movement desensitization and reprocessing) therapy that said most people feel better after only ten sessions!"

We do this because we want to help our partner. We want to cheerlead or coach our partners to feeling better. We want to feel connected to them again; we want to stop feeling so worried about them all the time.

You might notice that these conversations go well sometimes—and sometimes, your partner might shut down when you say these things. Or they might become defensive or upset. Your partner might have a hard time knowing that when you broach these conversations, you're trying to help or looking for reassurance. Instead of hearing your love and care for them, they might experience you as impatient or might feel like you're judging them, or they might even feel guilty that they haven't been able to get over their trauma. Sometimes survivors have an even harder time healing when it feels to them that they are a burden to their loved ones.

There are several things to keep in mind here. One is that if you sometimes feel burdened by your partner's trauma, this isn't something wrong for which you have to punish yourself. It's normal to feel frustrated by something that's difficult and keeps you distanced from someone you love. And ultimately, all feelings are valid. And what really matters is not the feelings you have, and whether they're right or wrong, but how you act on them, and the consequences these actions have. What's more, you clearly have a lot of love for your partner, as you're taking the time to read this book so that you can better understand how to help them get to a better place. It makes so much sense that you are looking for reassurance that you two are on the right track! That you and your partner are doing everything in your power to get to a better place. It is hard to go through suffering in our lives and relationships.

Let's take some time to consider the experience you and your partner are having with the tough conversations that might be coming up.

REFLECTION QUESTIONS

Does this pattern sound familiar to you?

How do you feel inside when you are wondering how long it might take for your partner to heal?

What are you afraid will happen if your partner doesn't "get better"?

Has anything been helpful when you have found yourselves in this pattern?

> *What would it be like to tell your partner about what you are feeling on the inside when it seems like you are impatient or judgmental about how they are feeling?*
>
> *How do you think your partner feels on the inside when you broach this topic with them?*

Feeling Angry at the Perpetrator

Gosh, is there anything more normal than feeling angry at the person who hurt someone we love? Anger is a healthy emotion when it is protective; it helps us gauge whether a person or situation is safe or whether boundaries need to be put in place. Sometimes, though, it feels like our anger is growing bigger than we can cope with. We might notice our thoughts turning toward our partner's perpetrator and how we wish we could seek revenge on them. It might feel like too much of our time is spent thinking about the perpetrator and how angry we are with them. We might feel a lot of pain over the fact that we can't express this anger at the harming person directly, or we might even feel frustrated if it seems like our partner isn't angry enough (in our opinion) at the person who traumatized them.

If anger is taking a toll on you, you might notice yourself feeling irritable in many situations, snapping at others in your life, or feeling emotionally exhausted. You might also be worried about whether your feelings are healthy or normal if you are noticing that you are wishing you could hurt the perpetrator in some way.

If you've expressed this anger to your partner, they may have seemed to understand—or they may have become worried that you would confront their perpetrator. In this situation, you might find it confusing that your partner doesn't want you to stand up for them or try to protect them. Or you might feel confused or feel like your partner doesn't trust you to make good decisions; after all, just because you might wish you could confront their perpetrator doesn't mean you'd actually do it if you had the opportunity.

Your traumatized partner might be overwhelmed with your anger, even if it's directed at an "appropriate" person. Anger can be a difficult emotion for survivors to experience in themselves and in others because it can feel like an unsafe emotion or one that can't be trusted.

Your partner will be able to process their own anger, if they have any, in their own time, but know that it is okay that you are experiencing anger if it is showing up for you! It's usually a sign that we need a sense of safety. And again, it's less *what* you're feeling that matters than how you deal with that feeling.

REFLECTION QUESTIONS

Have you noticed anger coming up for you?

What is anger like for you to feel and how do you usually express it (if you do)?

Has your anger caused tension in your relationship with your partner as they try to heal?

Has anything you've done when this comes up been helpful? What kinds of things seem to help you feel safer when you are angry?

How do you think your partner feels on the inside when you express anger toward their perpetrator?

Encouraging Your Partner to Get Therapy or Try Medication

If you are someone who embraces getting support when you're struggling, you may have brought up ways your partner can seek their own support for their trauma. Sometimes our partners are open to seeing a therapist or trying medication for their symptoms, but sometimes they may be scared or not ready to do so. When we bring up starting therapy or talking to their doctor about mental health medication, we often do it because we believe these methods are helpful. We care about our partners and want to make sure they have all the support they need to feel better. Sometimes, especially when someone is either wary of therapy or medication or scared to open up about their trauma, they can hear our expression of support as us telling them they are overreacting or need to go fix themselves.

This is probably not your intention at all, and it can be hard to hear your partner respond in this way. If you have had these conversations with your partner and they haven't gone well, you might be feeling hurt that they rejected your offer of help, frustrated that they aren't seeking help that could get them to a better place, or really worried about them! All of these feelings make sense in this situation.

> ### REFLECTION QUESTIONS
> Have you brought up therapy or trying medication to your partner? If so, how did it go?
> What are you worried will happen if they don't seek support in these ways?
> Have there been times in your life when you knew you needed help but were scared to get it?
> How do you think your partner felt when you discussed this topic with them?

Wanting Your Partner to Involve Law Enforcement or Explore Legal Options

Sometimes when we know our partner has been sexually assaulted or abused, we want to see justice for them in the form of their perpetrator having to face a consequence.

There are many reasons why a survivor might not feel comfortable involving law enforcement or pressing charges, but even with many valid reasons it can still be hard for you, as their loved one, to accept that their perpetrator "is getting away with it" or is not facing any punishment for the harm they did. There might be something about seeing a "bad guy" have to face the consequences of their actions that can bring us a sense of relief or even a sense of safety—protecting our partner and others from their dangerous behavior. If you are someone who has a general trust for the legal system or finds peace in consequences and justice, it might feel confusing and frustrating if your partner declines to make a report or become involved in an investigation or legal proceedings.

Ultimately, this—whether to involve law enforcement or the legal system in the prosecution of a crime—is your partner's decision to make, not yours. It's also true that our institutions don't always treat victims well—and this is a factor for many survivors as they consider whether they want to engage the legal system or not. But it can be very hard to not get a say. So, you may find yourself encouraging them to take action or even pressuring them to do so.

Again, this makes sense because you are scared. You want to protect your loved one from this ever happening again. You want to believe you can create safety for your loved one or others—you also are mad at the perpetrator and want them to be punished.

Sometimes your partner might be open to these conversations and really want to know your opinions as they try to decide what to do. Other times, they might feel pressured or judged by you—and then they may pull away or become frustrated with you. They might not feel understood by you, and it can create more disconnection in the relationship. This is the last thing you want to happen because you want to protect your partner and feel close to them.

REFLECTION QUESTIONS

Have you encouraged your partner to involve law enforcement or take part in legal proceedings? If so, how did it go?

What are you worried will happen if they don't file a report or press charges?

Have there been times in your life when you were afraid to seek support from the justice system?

How do you think your partner felt when you discussed this topic with them?

Worrying Your Partner Will Be Assaulted Again

Are you worried your partner will be assaulted again? It's normal if your thoughts turn to how you can keep an assault from happening again, particularly if the assault was recent. This is a common experience of us humans: a bad thing happens and we try to stop it from happening in the future. It's also common to feel guilty that we weren't there to protect our partners or angry at others who failed to protect them. We might even start focusing on what our partner could have done to avoid the sexual assault in the first place.

People who have been traumatized (and as a survivor's partner you are included in this) sometimes feel hypervigilant. They start noticing and fixating on things that pose a threat. This has a very protective component—if we become more aware of our environment, we may be able to keep ourselves safe. You might notice that you feel compelled to remind your partner to stay safe, to ask them about what they could have done differently to stay safe, to encourage them to avoid situations that you perceive as unsafe. You might notice that it's not only hard to trust the world to keep your loved one safe, but it's also hard to trust your partner to keep themself safe. Again, your feelings make sense. You are scared and trying to create safety and security for your partner and, in doing so, yourself and your relationship.

As for your partner, they might feel supported when you remind them to stay safe and avoid dangerous situations—and sometimes doing everything you can to keep your partner safe is the best thing you can do. But exploring this topic with your partner can also cause tension. They may feel overwhelmed by your anxiety or even like you're victim blaming—seeing them as part of the reason the assault happened. This is probably the last thing that you want to do! You don't want your partner to feel at fault for the horrible things that happened to them, and you're just hoping for their own sake that it doesn't happen again—and trying to help them make decisions that will stop it from doing so. But it's necessary to know that your partner may justifiably feel judged, blamed, or defensive when these conversations happen. This may cause them to pull away, become angry with you, and have a harder time forgiving themself, if they do blame themself at all for their trauma. Many survivors do blame themselves, even when they can objectively recognize that what happened to them was not their fault. Ultimately, it's best to find ways to deal with the anxiety and stress you feel that *don't* run the risk of compounding your partner's stress and trauma.

REFLECTION QUESTIONS

> *Do these feelings or conversations sound familiar to you?*
>
> *How do you feel inside when you are trying to keep your partner safe through suggestions, questions, or tips on staying safe?*
>
> *What are you afraid will happen if you don't give your partner advice on staying safe?*
>
> *Has anything been helpful when you have had these conversations?*
>
> *What would it be like to tell your partner about what you are feeling on the inside when they communicate that they feel like you are victim blaming or giving unsolicited advice?*
>
> *How do you think your partner feels on the inside when you broach this topic with them?*

Having Your Own Trauma Retriggered

When we are survivors of abuse or violence, we may find ourselves triggered by our partner's story of sexual trauma, whether or not our own trauma was of a sexual nature. Seeing your partner heal from trauma might bring up your own memories of trauma, suffering, and healing. You may become emotionally overwhelmed, have your own PTSD triggered, or identify so closely with their experience that it is hard to support them the way you want to.

First of all, if you are experiencing this, I am so sorry that you are being impacted in this way. I hope that you have your own support system to turn to or self-care rituals that help you when your trauma is triggered.

I know from working with couples where both partners are survivors that there can be deep levels of connection and bonding—feeling like they really "get" each other. Your partner may find some comfort in knowing that you are also a survivor of trauma; they may feel relieved to know that some of the ways they are feeling make total sense to you because you have felt those feelings as well. On the other hand, it also might be overwhelming to you and your partner to have both of you becoming triggered or re-experiencing traumatic memories at the same time; this can make connection and understanding each other hard in times of distress.

REFLECTION QUESTIONS

If you are a survivor of abuse or violence, have you been triggered by hearing about your partner's experiences?

How do you feel inside when you are triggered or experiencing flashbacks or trauma symptoms, and what seems to help ground or soothe you?

Do you feel like you have people or places to turn to when you need support?

Wondering Whether Your Partner Is Overreacting

It's happened again. You said something or you touched your partner a certain way or they had a flashback, and now they've had a big emotional response or they're completely shut down. You love your partner and know they are in pain. But part of you whispers inside, *Are they overreacting? Does it make sense that they are still being affected so strongly?*

You know from what we learned in chapter 1 that trauma can stay with us for a very long time, and that all of your partner's feelings are valid. But you still might find yourself overwhelmed when your partner has a strong trigger response and you would like them to be able to find other ways to cope.

You might bring this up to your partner, too. But sometimes, even if you've tried to broach the topic in the most delicate and loving way, your partner may become hurt, defensive, or angry with you. They may tell you they don't feel understood, that they feel judged by you or pushed to get better. They often are also judging themselves in the same way and angry with themselves for having such a strong emotional reaction when they are triggered, and they may share that because of this they are very hurt that you have the same thoughts.

It makes sense that you want to know your partner is having a normal reaction because you want them to feel better. You want to know that one day you'll be able to be connected and intimate with them without their trauma being triggered. It might feel like their trauma is a third party in your relationship, and it might feel like their trauma gets in the way of moments that could instead bring more love, enjoyment, and pleasure to your relationship.

REFLECTION QUESTIONS

Do these feelings or conversations sound familiar to you?

How do you feel inside when you're wondering whether your partner is overreacting?

What are you afraid will happen if your partner continues to be triggered or have the symptoms they are experiencing?

Has anything been helpful when you have had these conversations?

If you know that your partner is not overreacting and their feelings and reactions are normal, how might you be able to cope when you become overwhelmed by their triggers or symptoms?

Scared to Trigger Your Partner or That They'll See You as a Perpetrator

When your partner has been traumatized by another person, you may carry some fear that they may see you as aggressive, someone who doesn't respect their boundaries and need for consent, or someone who otherwise causes them distress and upset.

As you move toward your partner for connection, they may become overwhelmed or triggered. This is a possible dynamic in all relationships because we are not able to read our partners' minds and know exactly how they'd like us to connect with them at any given time.

If you have ever triggered your partner, you may have felt overwhelmed yourself, scared of hurting them in that moment or in the future, or even frustrated that it appears to you that they do not feel safe in your presence. It makes sense if these feelings come up for you because loving your partner and keeping them safe is very important to you. When it feels like they're scared of you or uncomfortable being close to you, you might feel rejected or like you are being lumped into the same category that their perpetrator is in—an unsafe person.

Your partner may have a hard time expressing how they feel in these moments, giving you reassurance, or letting you know what they need because their bodies and minds automatically go into a trauma response. When this pattern pops up, it can feel isolating for each of you, as you feel helpless in response to the trauma triggers that keep you from being close with each other.

> ### REFLECTION QUESTIONS
> *Does this pattern sound familiar to you?*
> *How do you feel inside when you trigger your partner or it seems like they are scared of you?*
> *Has anything been helpful when you have found yourselves in this pattern?*
> *What would it be like to tell your partner that you are worried you scare them?*
> *How do you think your partner feels on the inside when they are triggered by you?*

Worried You Won't Be Able to Be Close to Your Partner Again

One of the most common concerns I hear from the clients I support is that they are worried they may not be able to be close to their partner physically and emotionally again (or even for the first time) if their partner is a sexual trauma survivor and having symptoms that make connection difficult in a relationship. This fear can fill you with grief and sadness as you so want to feel that connection and closeness that relationship intimacy provides. There can be nothing like expressing and receiving love through emotional and physical connection.

When you are worried that this isn't possible in your relationship, you may try many things to make the situation better—including a lot of the behaviors and experiences we've explored in this chapter. If you don't see improvement in the situation or you begin to lose hope, you might even consider ending the relationship altogether. This can bring up guilt and sadness because you likely don't want to lose the relationship; you just feel very lonely and scared that nothing will get better.

If you have explored these feelings with your partner, they may have started feeling more pressure to "get over" the trauma, and this can be a struggle for them if they are doing the best they can. They may feel guilt or fear of losing you, or they may begin to feel hopeless in the relationship as well. These feelings can be very hard to reckon with, and it's at this point that partners often reach out for therapy or turn to resources such as this book.

REFLECTION QUESTIONS

Do these feelings sound familiar to you?

Have you and your partner discussed these feelings and fears? If so, how has it gone?

Has anything been helpful when these fears come up?

> *What would it be like to tell your partner how much they mean to you and that you are afraid of losing them?*
>
> *Do you know whether your partner feels the same way?*

I hope that hearing about common experiences and feelings for people in similar situations as you is helping you feel less alone. It can be very isolating to be struggling as we worry about our partner and our relationship. We may feel like no one understands what we are going through.

While the second half of this book will focus on tips and exercises to support your partner and improve your relationship, these first chapters are meant to help you understand your experiences and begin to become more aware of the patterns and feelings that are causing you and your partner distress.

In the next section, we will refresh our memories on common relationship attachment styles and behaviors. We will also begin to map how these attachment styles are showing up in our relationships. This will lay the groundwork to help you understand where you are getting stuck in your dance toward relationship connection. You will also get guidance on which new skills and relationship exercises might be most helpful to improve your relationship connection and your ability to support your partner.

Your and Your Partner's Attachment Styles

In chapter 1, we reviewed relationship attachment styles and looked at some examples. Our attachment styles play a major role in how we handle stress within our relationships and in the cycle of disconnection that often occurs in times of relationship distress. In the following exercises, I invite you to explore how these factors impact you, your partner, and your relationship.

EXERCISE: Identifying Your Attachment Style in Times of Distress

This exercise will help you identify which attachment style you and your partner might default to when either of you is in distress. Of course, we don't always move through the world consistently in one attachment style. For this exercise, it will be helpful to think about times that you or your partner has felt either triggered or unsafe due to the trauma. It will also help to consider times that you or your partner has felt the relationship has been threatened by disconnection, arguments, or other ways that your partner's sexual trauma might put stress on your relationship. With that in mind, read the descriptions below and notice where each of you most often lands in times of distress. It's possible that you have a mix of styles, but it's more likely that one pattern seems to cause the most conflict or pain in the relationship. (Although these are written in first-person point of view, consider how these apply to both you and your partner.)

Secure attachment: In times of relationship distress, I tend to...

☐ want to understand what my partner is thinking and feeling so I can better support them.

☐ feel comfortable or at least know the importance of opening up to my partner about how I am feeling, even when it feels vulnerable to do so.

☐ understand that conflict is inevitable in a relationship and remain hopeful even in times of distress.

☐ express emotional needs and wants in the relationship, and accept that my partner won't always be able to meet these needs.

☐ strive to meet my partner's emotional needs whenever I can, and see them as important.

☐ accept that I won't always be able to meet my partner's needs, but will provide reassurance and nurturing when my partner needs it.

☐ generally trust my partner and can come back to repair the relationship when things do not go well.

Avoidant attachment: In times of relationship distress, I tend to...

☐ shut down or withdraw when triggered or overwhelmed.

☐ worry about letting my loved ones down or that I am "not enough" or "never good enough."

☐ feel anxious or panicked when I feel pressured to address an issue or uncomfortable situation in the moment or when I don't know what to say.

☐ feel scared that I will not be understood or accepted by others if I am open with them.

☐ sometimes show anger, frustration, or sadness when I feel pressured to talk about something that makes me feel overwhelmed or uncomfortable.

☐ want to be able to pause or stop uncomfortable situations; may even pull away or shut down in order to do so.

Anxious attachment: In times of relationship distress, I tend to...

☐ want to talk about things immediately and sometimes push to have tough discussions even when my partner isn't open to doing so.

☐ feel anxious or panicked that an issue or uncomfortable situation isn't resolved quickly or doesn't have a clear answer about what to do to make things better.

☐ sometimes show anger, frustration, or sadness when my partner wants to end a tough conversation or does not contribute to the conversation (shuts down, withdraws).

☐ like to give feedback or suggestions in the hopes that it will be helpful or improve the relationship.

☐ share my opinions and some or most of my feelings.

☐ feel abandoned, dismissed, or rejected sometimes in my relationship or feel like I am "too much."

Disorganized attachment: In times of relationship distress, I tend to...

☐ experience extreme emotional reactions and a mix of anxious and avoidant responses in my relationships.

When you reflect on these attachment styles, which style seems most like you? Which style seems most like your partner?

As we begin to shed light on our attachment styles and the patterns they create, we will draw from an approach called emotionally focused couples therapy (EFT), which was developed by Sue Johnson (Johnson 2015). EFT views relationship dynamics through the lens of attachment, and practitioners of EFT believe that understanding the layers of our attachment patterns and finding new ways to express ourselves in these patterns enables us to create more secure attachment bonds. As you'll recall from chapter 1, it's the relationships we have with our caregivers and those closest to us that determine how we relate to others and ourselves going forward. Close relationships in which we're nurtured and loved leave us better able to nurture and love ourselves and deal adaptively with whatever we might face in life. This means that when we feel more secure in our relationship, we often feel more secure in the world around us and are better able to address stressful or even traumatic situations. And it's significant because while the trauma your partner experienced is external to the relationship, the security you create in distressing moments within your relationship can both help improve your relationship and help your partner heal from their trauma.

In the previous exercise, you identified the attachment style and behaviors you typically default to during times of relationship distress. These behaviors often create a disconnection cycle within relationships, where partners' differing attachment styles lead to increasing conflict. For example, a common disconnection cycle is one where one partner has a more anxious attachment style and one partner has a more avoidant attachment style. The partner with the anxious attachment style may be more vocal or direct when trying to connect with their loved one, and this may overwhelm the partner with the avoidant attachment style, so they begin to shut down. The anxious partner continues to pursue connection (but may seem angry to the avoidant partner) as the avoidant partner tries to calm the cycle by remaining quiet or removing themselves, which, in turn, triggers the anxious partner to become more distressed that they are losing connection in the relationship. As you can see, this cycle can go around and around as both partners become more overwhelmed. By exploring the underlying emotions and thoughts each person is having, we can begin to better understand each other. The following chapters will include more skills that help deescalate these painful cycles.

Let's turn to another exercise to explore how this might play out in your own relationship.

EXERCISE: Exploring Your Relationship Disconnection Cycle

In this exercise, we will map out the various factors contributing to your and your partner's cycle of disconnection. To do this, I'll ask you to reflect on the behaviors you default to in your relationship, the emotions that drive these behaviors, the unmet emotional needs you may have, the positive intention that may lie behind your behaviors, the impact of your behaviors on your partner, how your partner responds, and what you might try instead to create more security in your relationship and more genuinely enable both your and your partner's needs to be met. I know that sounds like a lot, so we'll break it down and take it slowly. You might complete these reflections on your own or with your partner if they are open to doing so. It is possible to make positive change even if you reflect on this on your own—as long as you are able to focus on what is in your own power to change. This often entails vulnerably opening up more to our partners and practicing our own behavioral changes while staying as open, nonjudgmental, and hopeful as we can about how our partners might respond to these changes.

Begin by reflecting on a recent time of disconnection in your relationship. Imagine that you are watching the two of you in this moment as if your interaction is on a movie screen in front of you. What happens? What do each of you do or say in this time of disconnection? Oftentimes, regardless of what exactly set the moment off, our disconnection cycle becomes familiar to us as a common pattern in times of distress—so we just go through it; we don't really observe it to see precisely what's happening, or how we might intervene in the cycle.

Write out the pattern now, as you see it. It will sound like a story of the interaction. If your partner participates in this activity, they will write out the pattern as well. It is okay if the two of you see some things differently in the pattern. You both have your own perspective. It's helpful to know each other's perspectives, though, so if you are doing this activity together, you might share the patterns you notice with each other. Notice which parts you see similarly.

It may read something like "When I can tell something is wrong with my partner, I ask them how they're feeling. My partner then looks at me with an angry face and tells me they don't want to talk about it. Then I become sad and tell them that they never want to talk about anything. They usually walk away at this point, and I usually follow them to the other room and ask them what I can do to help them feel better. They tell me they need to be by themself and ask me to leave the room. I go sit in the living room and don't know what to do at that point. I don't bring it up later with my partner because I don't want to have another argument, but it doesn't feel like anything was resolved or that they want to open up to me. It feels like they don't like me very much in these moments."

Now we will identify the layers of these moments by becoming more familiar with the behaviors (or actions), emotions, and thoughts that arise when this pattern shows up.

Behaviors/Actions

Behaviors are what we do. All our behaviors usually have a positive intention related to trying to get our needs met—even if that need is just to be heard or to express the strong feelings we're having, however we feel able. Sometimes what we do in times of distress to get our needs met confuses or hurts our partner even when we don't mean for it to do so. This is what contributes to these patterns of disconnection going around and around without having a resolution. But often, even when we don't like a behavior that we have or can rationally understand why it is harmful, it can be hard to stop or change the behavior. That is because our behaviors are so closely intertwined with our feelings and thoughts that they become automatic—especially when we are trying to get our relationship attachment needs met.

In times of distress, what behaviors do you use to get your needs met? Do you move toward or away from your partner? Here are some common relationship behaviors that occur in times of distress:
- shutting down, withdrawing
- asking questions, asking the same questions repeatedly
- criticizing
- blaming
- looking for the "bad guy"
- defending your own case, explaining yourself
- giving advice
- yelling
- intellectualizing

- playing therapist or psychoanalyzing your partner
- interrupting your partner
- changing the subject
- bringing up other complaints

When you do the behaviors you identified above, you are most likely doing them to try to get a very important need met. You might be trying to
- connect with your partner,
- feel loved by your partner,
- feel understood,
- feel safe,
- stop uncomfortable feelings, or
- protect yourself from hurting.

These are the positive intentions of your behavior. Which ones do you most identify as representative of what you are trying to do when you act a certain way?

Even though your behaviors are aimed at helping you get your needs met and feel closer to your partner, they may have the opposite effect in the moment. How does your partner seem to respond when you behave in the ways you identified above? Do they move toward you or away from you? They are likely influenced in these moments by their attachment style, just as your behaviors are influenced by yours.

Look back on the behavior list you reviewed above. What behaviors or reactions does your partner tend to have?

Emotions

Emotions are how we feel in these moments. It's normal to feel multiple ways at the same time—and some emotions are more overwhelming to us or our partners than others. Sometimes we might feel like our emotions don't make sense or we wish we didn't feel this way. Sometimes it feels like someone is making us feel an emotion that we don't like. These uncomfortable experiences of our own emotions are closely related to how we act in these moments of disconnection.

Emotions, even the ones that feel "bad," are actually helpful to us. They help us know what we need and can motivate us to seek loving connection to soothe ourselves. This is also why it can be so painful when it feels like our partner doesn't understand our emotions or when we have a hard time communicating them in a way that facilitates connection instead of conflict.

Having an emotional vocabulary is helpful as you begin to understand your disconnection cycle and find new ways of connecting.

Here are some common emotions you may feel in times of disconnection:
- angry, mad, frustrated
- panicked, scared, overwhelmed, anxious
- sad, hurt
- embarrassed, guilty, ashamed
- betrayed, violated, attacked
- judged, criticized

- defensive, protective
- helpless, powerless

Which emotions in this list are most resonant for you? Which are most resonant for your partner? (If you're doing this exercise alone, do your best to recall or imagine what your partner might be feeling—with the understanding, of course, that this is your best guess.)

Thoughts

Another layer of our disconnection cycle is the thoughts we are having inside when we find ourselves in this pattern again with our partner. These thoughts may be opinions we have of our partner and what they are doing, or opinions or fears we have about ourselves or the relationship, now or in the future. Sometimes we share these thoughts out loud and sometimes we only think them inside.

Some examples of thoughts you may have when you are triggered into your cycle of disconnection:

- *They will never stop making me feel this way.*
- *They don't care about me.*
- *They don't love me anymore.*
- *I'm a bad partner.*
- *I'm unlovable.*
- *They don't understand me.*
- *We will never get to a better place.*

Sometimes we hook into, or overidentify with, these thoughts as if they are the end-all, be-all truth. We can feel very stuck when we hook into these thoughts. Most of the time these thoughts are scary and cause us to feel more distressed in the moment. When we feel those distressing feelings we identified above, we automatically react with the behaviors we identified above. This is how our emotions, behaviors, and thoughts are all connected and can keep us stuck in painful patterns.

If you are working though this exercise with your partner, it is helpful to first reflect on your own answers to better understand yourself. Then, if you are open to discussing it together, you can do so. Sometimes sharing your answers is too painful or your partner isn't ready to participate yet. That is okay. You will learn more skills in future chapters to help you two connect about these experiences, thoughts, and feelings.

If you do decide to share what you've learned about yourselves with each other, try to do so from the perspective of better understanding each other, not yet trying to change or fix anything. The goal is just to understand what is really going on inside our partner when they are acting a certain way. When we see that it is coming from a place of pain and fear of losing connection with us, it can improve our ability to feel empathy and decrease our own pain and defensiveness. This is the foundation of building connection and secure bonding in a relationship.

If you and your partner are not ready to share these understandings with each other, it can still be helpful to find ways to process your feelings and what you've learned. You might journal about what you've learned in this chapter, discuss your thoughts and feelings with a therapist, or even create artwork to represent what you are feeling inside. All of these activities can help you externally process and move through your emotions.

Putting It All Together

I hope that by reading this chapter you are starting to feel less alone with your feelings and experiences. It is hard to navigate your own pain while also trying to be there for your partner. Sometimes the feelings or urges you have get in the way of helping to meet your partner's needs. This can create a cycle of disconnection for both of you and additional pain in the relationship. In the next chapter, you'll discover how investing in your relationship and how you show up to support your partner can both help your partner heal and increase your own satisfaction in your relationship.

CHAPTER 3

Your Relationship as a Source for Healing

Now that we've spent time understanding the different ways sexual trauma can impact survivors, their partners, and the relationship, it's important to instill hope that things can get better! One of the most impactful ways that people heal from trauma is by building a sense of security and connection in their important relationships. This chapter will explain the important role you play in your partner's healing and show that it is possible for both partners to come together and build a secure bond that benefits each person in their healing and beyond.

We will continue to use the frame of relationship attachment theory throughout this chapter and also add activities on mindful self-compassion, stress management skills, and relationship boundaries. All of the information and tips provided in this chapter will help you facilitate healing by building a secure relationship and self-concept.

Let's first get a better understanding of how sexual trauma is a type of relational trauma that can be healed within the context of a secure relationship with a trusted partner.

Relational Trauma

Relational trauma is any trauma or abuse experienced at the hands of another person. When we experience a natural disaster trauma such as a wildfire, our trauma symptoms may cause us to fear that we aren't safe in our homes and that our environment may take away our sense of safety at any time. When our trauma is experienced at the hands of another person, our trauma symptoms may cause us to fear other people, leaving us with a belief that other people may take away our sense of safety at any time.

This becomes complex when we are trying to connect with people we have trusted in the past or to build new relationships. Even if the people we want to connect with are not the perpetrators of the abuse, the perpetrators left a lasting impact on us that may affect our ability to get close to other people.

Returning to the wildfire example, a survivor of a wildfire who lost their home in the annual wildfires in my home state of California may have symptoms of PTSD. They may choose to remove themself from living in an environment that is at a higher risk for fires. If a friend of ours survived a wildfire and then told us they are choosing to move to a town with a very low risk of wildfire, this would make sense to us, right? We'd see that as a logical decision based on their experience and the reality of the world.

In the same way, a survivor of sexual trauma may feel with every fiber of their being that they need to remove themself from risky situations. They may avoid sexual connection, romantic relationships, or environments similar to the one in which they experienced the trauma. This becomes more complicated than the choice in the wildfire example, though, because human beings are wired to need and build relationships for safety, connection, and pleasure. Relationships, a basic human need, become scary and overwhelming—and this happens at the same time that the survivor of sexual trauma needs relationships most for comfort and security, a time when they're suffering with an intensely painful and isolating experience.

For those of us who are partners of sexual trauma survivors, we might see our partners both need us and feel scared of relationships with us at the same time. This is confusing to our partners and confusing to us—but in the context of relationship trauma, it actually makes a lot of sense. Our partners' instincts and bodies are telling them to move toward us at the same time they are telling them to isolate and disconnect from others. It makes sense that their feelings and behaviors are confusing!

Now the hopeful part.

Those of us closest to a survivor of sexual trauma (or any relational trauma, really) are actually best placed to help our partners heal from their trauma. Survivors of sexual trauma can relearn or develop a sense of safety through positive relationship experiences with trusted people. That's you, if you choose to support them!

Your partner has been coping with a painful traumatic experience, and you are taking the time to read a book to better understand them and how to support them. This is huge. You are already taking action to be a person who supports your partner's healing in a significant way.

Sometimes you will feel overwhelmed and those feelings of helplessness may come up. Remind yourself that showing up for your partner—even when it doesn't seem to go well, even when they continue to hurt and you do as well—is the greatest thing you can do to support them and improve your relationship.

As we discussed in chapter 2, creating and maintaining a secure bond in your relationship, even in moments of distress, is helpful in supporting your partner in their healing. And it's helpful regardless of what your partner is going through—but especially when it relates to relational trauma. You are showing them through their experiences with you that they can feel safe in a relationship with another person, and that even when there are times of conflict or moments of distress, they will be respected and cared about by you.

Being a support person to a partner with trauma can also take a toll on you. You may feel pressure to get it right, your own emotions and relationship traumas can be triggered, and you may become burned out if you don't take care of yourself. The next sections of this chapter will look at how you can take care of yourself while showing up for your partner—by using elements of mindful self-compassion to help regulate your own emotions, by practicing self-care and stress reduction to keep you from burning out, and by establishing healthy boundaries that protect each partner in the relationship. Read on to learn more about each of these ways of coping.

Mindful Self-Compassion

Although practicing compassion toward ourselves is not a new concept, Kristen Neff has spearheaded recent research and evidence-based practices in this area. Practicing compassion toward ourselves in times of distress has been shown to help us accept and soothe our painful emotions, comfort ourselves, and become resilient so that we may continue to make decisions and take actions that are in line with our values in life (Neff 2012).

As you've likely experienced at some point in your life, receiving compassion and kindness from others can help you feel less alone, not give up when you are faced with something hard, see different perspectives, and refrain from becoming stuck in your suffering. Mindful self-compassion is the practice of internally giving yourself these same benefits. And the practice of mindful self-compassion can support you as you support your partner.

Neff (2012) has identified three key elements of self-compassion: (1) self-kindness (as opposed to self-judgment); (2) knowledge of the common humanity you share with others at all times, no matter how difficult your experience (as opposed to isolation and a sense that you must be the only one experiencing the pain you're feeling); and (3) mindfulness and the ability to see your feelings as information (as opposed to overidentification with your feelings, such that they launch you into automatic behaviors that may do more harm than good). I will describe and give examples of the three components of mindful self-compassion and offer exercises to help you practice the techniques.

Self-Kindness vs. Self-Judgment

When we are going through a hard time, we might be quick to judge ourselves or feel ashamed by how we acted or felt. When we are able to be kind to ourselves even when we feel we should have done something differently, we are much less likely to get stuck in shame or prolonged suffering.

This might have come up as you were reading previous information in this book. Maybe after learning more about your partner's experience and what they are needing, you regret ways you've acted in the past. It's okay to not get it right every time! No one does. Our own life experiences inform how we act in any situation, and no human moves through the world "perfectly" avoiding conflict, helping all situations improve, and never hurting the people we love.

We can use self-compassion here instead of hurting or judging ourselves for things we think we got wrong. Let's look at how our friend Todd might do this.

You'll recall that Todd began to feel ashamed of himself when he realized that he had been dismissive of his wife and the many survivors of sexual trauma. And as he learned more about sexual trauma and rape culture, he realized that he had been complicit and maybe even a perpetrator through victim blaming, laughing along with friends at misogynistic jokes, and pressuring a former partner for sex in a previous relationship. He ended up feeling so ashamed that he wasn't sure what to do.

If Todd is feeling frozen in his shame and berating himself, he may not be able to make repairs with his loved ones and make positive change in his life and in our world. Instead of hating himself over his prior actions, he might practice self-compassion by speaking to himself in a loving way: *You weren't aware of how* damaging your past behaviors were, and now that you are, it's okay to feel guilty and want to do better. You were raised within rape culture and have been practicing the same beliefs and behaviors that were modeled to you by the media, your communities, and your peers. By listening to Jennifer and being open to survivor stories, you are learning new ways to be in the world. You can make a difference and try new ways of being even though you regret the ways you've acted in the past. It's okay to make mistakes.

What do you notice as Todd speaks to himself in this way? What would it be like to speak to yourself in this way?

EXERCISE: Practicing Self-Kindness

I'd like to invite you to practice self-kindness. Start by reflecting on ways you've responded to your partner as they heal from sexual trauma. Next, identify one thing you wish you had done differently now that you have a better understanding of your partner's experience and needs.

Notice any negative, self-blaming thoughts you speak to yourself (this is the unhelpful self-judgment). Now imagine that you were speaking to yourself with loving-kindness, the same way you would speak to someone you love with compassion, kindness, and encouragement. Write out the way you might give yourself

self-compassion, in the same way Todd was able to give himself self-compassion.

Know that it's okay if your self-compassion doesn't feel totally true to you. This is an active practice that becomes more soothing the more we practice it.

Common Humanity vs. Isolation

Neff identifies the second component of mindful self-compassion as common humanity instead of isolation. When we are struggling, we often believe that there is something wrong with us, that we are the only ones experiencing this pain. When we feel this way, we pull back from others and avoid connection because we fear being judged or rejected. We also have a hard time moving forward because we feel helpless in our shame and pain.

We are not alone in our pain and suffering. Avoiding suffering in life is impossible because suffering is a universal human experience. We all make mistakes; things don't go the way we want them to; people hurt us; we become disappointed in others, ourselves, and the world. When we practice common humanity, we are reminding ourselves that we are not alone in our experience and that pain is a given in life.

Let's look at how this applies to Thomas and Marina.

Thomas and Marina have been struggling particularly hard to connect since Marina gave birth. She's feeling triggered by the pressure she feels to reconnect with Thomas emotionally and physically even though she is exhausted by having an infant to care for. And Thomas feels rejected by Marina again and again. He is frustrated that she does not seem to be making an effort to connect with him, and he also starts to worry something's wrong with him. He is in a lot of pain.

Thomas may find himself thinking he's alone in this experience because all the other couples he sees seem to have it so much easier than they do. He might tell himself that other partners don't go through such struggles, or that it should be easier for him and Marina to reconnect intimately after becoming parents. These beliefs may prolong or exacerbate his pain.

Practicing common humanity here may look like Thomas thinking to himself, *It makes sense that we are struggling right now. A lot of couples have a hard time reconnecting after having a child. It also makes sense that I'm hurting during this time because I feel more and more rejected and disappointed. It's hard for anyone when they want to feel close to their partners but there are barriers in the way.*

What do you notice might be helpful about this different way Thomas practices talking to himself with common humanity language? Note that the reassuring language Thomas uses is different from his telling himself that he *shouldn't* have to feel frustrated like this in his relationship and that couples *should* have an easy time reconnecting after becoming parents. He's not talking about what "should" happen; he's talking about what's happening to him and Marina, specifically, and telling himself that it makes sense and that it is normal for couples in their particular situation.

In the next exercise, you'll consider how you can practice common humanity in your own relationship.

EXERCISE: *Practicing Common Humanity*

Reflect on ways you've felt alone in times of distress or like things should be easier when you and your partner try to connect. Notice any ways you tell yourself things "should" be different or that you "shouldn't" have to feel the way you do.

Now imagine that you are speaking to yourself with the language of common humanity, connecting yourself and your experience to the common experiences couples have, or what you have learned is normal in relationships that have been impacted by sexual trauma. Write out the way you might speak to yourself with common humanity language, similar to how Thomas was able to do so.

Know that it's okay if your common humanity language doesn't feel totally true to you right now. This is an active practice that becomes more soothing the more we practice it.

Mindfulness vs. Overidentification

Neff identifies the third component of mindful self-compassion as mindfulness. We become most overwhelmed by our emotions when we hook into them. We might notice that instead of experiencing our emotions as helpful information and phenomena that come and go, we start experiencing our emotions as constant and representative of who we are. When this happens, it's harder to be open to different perspectives or try new ways of doing things. Because our emotions are so intertwined with our thoughts and behaviors, as we discussed in chapter 2, if our emotions are sustained or we become stuck in them, it is much harder to change our unhelpful thoughts and behaviors.

The way that we can improve this stuckness is through mindfulness. Mindfulness is a practice of noticing our feelings and thoughts without overidentifying with them. We can allow our feelings and thoughts to come and go, noticing how they change over time with different experiences.

Let's return to Gia and Samantha and see how mindfulness might be helpful to Samantha.

Gia and Samantha are hurting as Gia falls deeper into a depression and Samantha feels very stuck in her anger about what happened to Gia.

It makes sense that Samantha is angry! Gia was assaulted by a leader in her workplace, where she had every right to expect a safe environment. Now Gia and Samantha's lives and relationship may be forever changed by abuse that they had no say in.

But Samantha is also noticing that she can't shake her anger. It is disruptive to her life and functioning. She thinks about it all the time and fantasizes about acting out in harmful ways toward Gia's perpetrator. At this point, her feelings of anger are keeping her from other areas of her life that she usually enjoys, and she's much more irritable than usual. Gia even shared with her that she's starting to feel scared by Samantha's anger. It does appear that Samantha is beginning to overidentify with her emotion of anger as it becomes more and more a part of her experience in all moments of her life.

Practicing mindfulness here may look like Samantha noticing when anger is present, rather than simply feeling it, and then exploring it, with curiosity, rather than acting on it instinctively or trying to suppress or get rid of it. In such moments, she might think to herself, *It makes sense that anger is coming up for me. When I feel angry, I notice that my heart beats fast and I want to scream. Because I can't express this anger directly to Gia's perpetrator, I notice that the anger stays stuck in my body. It comes out in different ways throughout my day. My anger is telling me to do something. I notice that when I take a run or talk* to my therapist about my anger, the anger lessens. I'm better able to interact with loved ones and I notice other feelings, such as peace and connection in my body. Anger wants to help me protect Gia and our relationship and it's okay not to be angry all the time. Getting stuck in the anger can keep me from the good parts of life, so I will notice and feel the anger and take a helpful action, so that I can move through the anger and into other experiences in my day.

Do you see how this balanced approach to anger helps Samantha become less stuck in her suffering? How do you think this helps her? How might mindfulness help you in the context of your own relationship?

EXERCISE: Practicing Mindfulness

Take a few moments to contemplate your emotions. Are there emotions that you feel stuck in as you try to support your partner's healing? Do you feel like you overidentify with those emotions—like they're more a part of you than is useful for you and your partner, or more a part of you than you want them to be? Notice any ways the emotions in question are overwhelming you or taking over parts of your life or your ability to show up for your partner.

What would it be like to pause when this emotion arises and just notice it? Imagine that you are speaking to yourself with mindfulness language, approaching your emotion through balanced language as you notice how your emotions come and go, when you simply let them be there without jumping to act on them. Write out the way you might speak to yourself with mindfulness language, similar to how Samantha was able to do so.

Know that it's okay if your practice of mindfulness doesn't feel totally true to you or isn't helpful right away. Like self-kindness and common humanity, this is an active practice that becomes more soothing the more we practice it.

Mindful self-compassion is something that we can practice internally to soothe our uncomfortable feelings during stressful experiences. It also helps build resiliency as we commit to supporting our partner in their healing and taking steps to move in the direction of the connected relationship we want. Another way we can build resiliency is by managing our stress levels so that we do not burn out.

Stress Management and Avoiding Burnout

Stepping into a support role for our loved one can create high levels of stress for us and increase our chances of burning out. When we are burned out emotionally, it is hard to care for ourselves and also be supportive to our partner. I'm sure you've heard this common saying to caregivers, that just as the flight attendant says before every takeoff, in case of an emergency, first we have to put on our own oxygen mask before assisting anyone else. If we cannot function, we aren't going to be in our best place to support others.

What are some ways you can put your oxygen mask on so that you don't burn out?

First, reflect on the following questions to help you identify activities in your life that recharge you and bring you positive experiences.

> ### REFLECTION QUESTIONS
>
> *What hobbies have you practiced in the past that bring you peace and joy?*
>
> *Are there people in your life whom, after spending time together, you leave feeling recharged? Who are they and have you been spending time with them lately?*
>
> *How much rest and sleep do you tend to need when you feel your best, and is there anything getting in the way of giving you this much rest?*
>
> *What ways do you enjoy moving your body and/or getting outside?*
>
> *When you reflect upon your life, in what ways have you enjoyed creating things (e.g., art, building, making, growing, cooking)?*

When you reflected on the questions above, what came to mind? How might you be able to put some time or energy into one or two of the activities you identified?

Research shows that certain activities specifically help us resist burnout by ending the stress cycle, which takes a toll on our bodies and mind (Nagoski and Nagoski 2019). You're probably familiar with one part of the stress cycle, fight or flight, in which our body responds automatically to perceived threat or danger by preparing, physiologically, to fight or flee. The complete stress cycle is the pattern that is needed to take our nervous system from activated, into flight-or-fight responses, to a place of calm and peace. We are very likely, as humans living in the modern world, to have our nervous system activated frequently throughout the day, and sometimes we don't have methods in place to help deactivate the stress our body feels. This increases our chance of living with chronic stress, which also increases our chances of burning out.

When you burn out as a support person for your partner, a survivor of sexual trauma, you might notice yourself feeling exhausted, or irritable, or pulling away from your partner. You also might start noticing that you are losing compassion for them and what they experienced.

You can limit your chances of burning out and even start coming back from burnout altogether by practicing activities that process and release the stress you hold in your body. Nagoski and Nagoski (2019) identified six evidence-based ways to help you process and release your stress. I summarize them below.

Deep breathing: Deep and slow breaths soothe us and release stress because they signal to our bodies that we are safe enough to slow down and breathe. When we are triggered or stressed, we often notice changes to our breathing (short, shallow breaths), and this type of breathing keeps our nervous system activated. By breathing long and deep, we deactivate our nervous system response. You can try a technique called square-breathing to practice this: breathe in for a count of 4, hold for a count of 4, breathe out for a count of 4, hold for a count of 4, and repeat until you notice your body starting to relax.

Physical activity: Finding and incorporating a way of moving our bodies is a common way people cope with stress and decreases chances of burning out. You don't need to train for a marathon to reap the benefits here. What physical activity do you most enjoy? Noticing when your body is holding on to stress and then choosing to participate in a physical activity will help you metabolize and release that stress. You can also incorporate a regular workout so this becomes a reliable way of closing your stress cycle each day.

Laughter: Laughter, especially deep belly laughs, releases our stress naturally.

This might be laughing with our partners about an inside joke, watching a hilarious movie or stand-up routine, or getting a good laugh with other people close to us.

Affection: Physical touch—including hugs, a comforting handhold, a loving back rub, kissing, and sex—all can help us complete our stress cycles so that we can relax. When we are not able to receive physical affection from our partner or other loved one, cuddling and petting a pet also has a positive impact.

A cathartic cry: When we have a good cry, it releases hormones that soothe and relax us. Some people love a good cry in the therapy room with their therapist or when connecting with a loved one, and some can get it through a favorite movie, reading a book, or watching touching video clips online.

Creative expression: Earlier we reflected on ways we have enjoyed being creative. Expressing ourselves through art and creativity of any kind helps us express and release our emotions and decreases stress.

REFLECTION QUESTIONS

Think of a time when one of the activities above helped you manage your stress. How did

> *you feel before the activity and how did you feel after?*
>
> *Do you have a favorite activity or two from the list above?*
>
> *How might you remind yourself to incorporate these activities into your day-to-day life to help you cope as you support your partner?*

Managing your stress through these activities greatly reduces your chance of burning out. By not burning out, you can continue to show up for your partner while also taking care of yourself. Sometimes, you might notice you are close to your emotional limits or your partner may notice they are close to theirs. When this happens, it's important to be able to communicate with each other where your boundary is so that you can step back and utilize one of the coping skills we have addressed in this chapter.

Boundaries

Boundaries are important to our relationship with our partner in many of the same ways that boundaries are helpful for all relationships. Boundaries are the expectations and agreements we create for how we wish to be treated and to treat each other and what to expect—and in this way, they help us feel loved, safe, and respected in our relationships. When boundaries are not discussed or respected, we are much more likely to hurt each other or become resentful and disconnected.

Boundaries are especially important in a relationship with a sexual trauma survivor because their boundaries were violated during their sexual trauma. Your partner might be easily triggered when they feel their boundaries are intruded upon—this is why it's important that you clearly communicate in your relationship about your boundaries and reassure each other that it is okay to establish boundaries when needed.

Establishing boundaries with people we love can be especially difficult because we may feel like we are rejecting them and therefore feel guilty when communicating our limits. This is a common experience, and if you've felt this way, you are not alone! Even though it might be hard to set a boundary when you need one, boundaries are necessary to support your partner effectively and create safety for each of you.

To give you an idea of ways that boundaries might be helpful to set or discuss in your relationship, I'll use our example stories from chapter 1 to highlight ways the partners set boundaries or times it may have been helpful for them to try to do so.

Thomas and Marina

Thomas and Marina are coping with the changes in their relationship and change to their romantic connection since becoming parents. Thomas is having a hard time in the relationship because Marina hasn't had the energy for or interest in connecting emotionally or sexually. And he's coping in ways that, while understandable, don't really respect or show much genuine interest in Marina's boundaries because he's too preoccupied with his own needs—bringing up the topic to her repeatedly and making romantic gestures to no avail. Marina tells Thomas she feels too pressured and, when that doesn't change his behavior, begins to withdraw even more.

It might be helpful in this partnership for Marina and Thomas to have a frank discussion about what they each can and cannot expect from the other person during this time. Without a clear expectation, it is likely that Thomas will keep guessing how to pursue connection with Marina, and Marina will become more and more overwhelmed as Thomas feels more and more rejected. Because Marina is feeling triggered by the pressure she feels and relates it to her prior abusive relationship, where she experienced sexual trauma, it is important that she feels any boundaries she sets will be respected by Thomas.

One example of a boundary they can set might be Marina asking Thomas to stop pursuing her for sex or for spending time together at unpredictable times. Instead, they can ask Marina's sister to watch their child for one to two hours once a week and they can use this time together to reconnect. Marina might also communicate that she does want to re-establish sexual connection eventually, but that she'd like to start with talking and cuddling, without the pressure for intercourse until she's ready. Thomas might ask her how he can know whether she's ready, and they can decide together that he may broach this topic during this time together once a week, and Marina will do her best to communicate lovingly and openly about whatever she might be feeling.

How might this boundary discussion help both partners in the relationship?

Favor and Frank

Favor and Frank have gotten to the point that they are avoiding sex because they both feel bad about the way that Frank was triggered by Favor's touch while initiating sex. Even though they had a bonding conversation to better understand each other, they both feel awkward and hesitant to re-establish connection. They are both hurting and confused.

It might be helpful for Favor and Frank to sit down together one more time to speak openly about what's been going on and what they're both feeling and then agree on boundaries and expectations that may support their connection. It sounds like (from what we know about their inner worlds) they both miss connecting with each other sexually. Because

Frank is the sexual trauma survivor, Favor can ask him what boundaries he might need during sex. If Frank lets Favor know where he doesn't want to be touched or any triggers he wants to avoid, this can empower both of them. In this conversation, it would also help for Favor to let Frank know that he can tell Favor in the moment if anything ever feels uncomfortable or too much. That is, Favor would tell Frank that boundaries aren't just something they'll set now, but something that Frank can set or change at any time; Favor will always respect them. Now, Favor can have less fear that he will trigger Frank because he knows what not to do—and he knows that Frank feels empowered to tell him in the moment if things change. And Frank can feel safe in their connection and begin his trauma healing by having his boundaries respected and knowing he can enforce them at any time; Favor will respect them.

What might be the hardest part for Favor and Frank as they establish these boundaries?

Gia and Samantha

Gia and Samantha's story gave us a nice example of boundaries being set after the couple first struggled for a bit. In their couples therapy session, Gia communicates with Samantha that Samantha's anger about the assault and toward Gia's perpetrator is beginning to feel too overwhelming for Gia. And she asks Samantha to find ways to cope with this anger that aren't as scary for her. The couple agrees to continue working on this in couples therapy.

Even though Gia was scared about Samantha's anger and likely felt nervous about bringing it up, she was able to ask for what she needed in the relationship—especially with a supportive mediating presence, in the form of their therapist. Samantha might have felt guilty and misunderstood during this conversation, but—with a little mindfulness—she was able to put those feelings on hold to reassure Gia and find new ways of coping so that she could respect Gia's boundaries.

How might Samantha's response to Gia help Gia in her sexual trauma healing?

Jennifer and Todd

Todd has come a long way in his relationship with Jennifer. Initially, Todd dismissed Jennifer's thoughts and feelings about rape culture and didn't seem to understand her experience as a survivor. As he opened his heart and mind, he began to better understand his impact on others and even became worried as to whether a college sexual interaction with a girlfriend was consensual.

Now, Todd wants to reach out to this former girlfriend and apologize for his actions. He feels ashamed of himself and wants to make things right. While Todd's ex might appreciate hearing from him and knowing he's sorry after all these years, depending on how she is or isn't still impacted by her experience with Todd, she might not want anything to do with him. If she does look back on their experience together as non-consensual, she may become triggered when he reaches out to her. It is important that Todd respect any verbal or nonverbal cues he gets if he does decide to reach out. If she does not reach back out to him after he initially contacts her, this might be a boundary she is establishing through no contact. She does not owe it to Todd to communicate this to him, and it would be important that he doesn't keep pursuing a conversation.

Why might it be triggering for Todd's former girlfriend if he keeps contacting her when she doesn't reply?

Julia and Nico

Julia and Nico have decided to pursue sex therapy to help their relationship. Julia has noticed that she "checks out" or becomes dissociative during sex and wants help remaining present.

Julia and Nico's sex therapist will support them in communicating boundaries before, during, and after sex that will build safety for Julia in the sexual relationship. Even though Nico has not acted in an unsafe manner with Julia, Julia's sexual trauma of repeated sexual molestation throughout her childhood has established a strong association of sex and danger. Through boundaries, communication, trauma soothing techniques, and positive experiences, Julia can learn how it feels to feel safe during sex so she becomes less dissociative and more present in her connection. This can increase her own enjoyment of sex and help build a stronger connection between the partners.

How might it help with Julia's trauma healing if Nico is patient and supportive as they establish these boundaries and expectations?

REFLECTION QUESTIONS

What boundaries has your partner communicated with you? How have you responded to these boundaries?

Have there been times that boundaries in your relationship have been unclear, and would it be helpful to bring some clarification through discussion?

What might help you respect your partner's boundaries even when part of you feels hurt that they've set the boundary?

How can you let your partner know it is okay to communicate boundaries in the relationship?

Are there any boundaries you need in order to cope better in the relationship? How might you lovingly bring these up with your partner?

While boundaries can be difficult to establish at times, I hope you've seen through the example stories that they are an important part of sexual trauma healing. When your partner feels safe with you in your relationship, they are in a better position to move through their relational trauma.

When boundaries become draining to uphold or you get closer to burnout in your supportive partner role, it can be helpful to reconnect to the compassion and empathy you have for your partner. Sometimes compassion flows easily and you can wrap your partner up in your loving understanding like a warm embrace. Other times, you might have a harder time connecting to compassion or empathy because your lived experience may be quite different than the experience of your loved one. You may feel confused or even annoyed and judgmental about how they are reacting as they recover from their sexual trauma. The next section will focus on helping you increase your compassion and empathy so that you naturally have more understanding for their experience. This will help your partner feel more relaxed in your interactions, and it can also help you by limiting your own chance of being triggered by your partner's feelings and actions.

Building Compassion and Empathy for Your Partner

In chapter 1, we reviewed the research on sexual trauma, we read survivor stories about the impact of sexual trauma on relationships, and we identified common feelings sexual trauma survivors experience and ways of coping. Having this knowledge can help you better understand your partner and build compassion.

Even when you haven't been through the same experience as a loved one, you can try to build empathy by connecting to your loved one's feelings because you may have experienced similar feelings before. Empathy is an important emotion to experience toward your partner. It is different from sympathy or feeling bad for someone. Empathy is stepping into your partner's shoes and connecting to their emotional experience as if you have joined them in the experience. When your partner feels your empathy, they feel less alone—this helps increase their healing and helps build a secure attachment between you both.

You might already experience empathy and communicate this to your partner. That is wonderful! We can always grow our experience of empathy, and the exercise below, through journal reflections, aims to help you connect to feelings or experiences that will increase your empathy for your partner. If you become overwhelmed or triggered by any of the journal reflections, it might be helpful to take a pause and practice one of the coping skills you identified earlier in this chapter. You may come back to the reflection question when you are ready, or you might choose not to return. It is okay to take the space you need when trauma or emotionally triggering moments come up for you.

EXERCISE: Building Empathy

Write about a time you were betrayed by someone you trusted. What happened and how did you feel? How did you cope with the situation? When you think about this person now and what they did, how do you feel?

Write about a time you felt violated by someone. Maybe someone broke into your car and stole things, maybe your house was burgled, or someone you knew snooped in your phone or email. What happened and how did you feel? How did you cope with the situation? When you think about this experience now, how do you feel?

Write about a time you felt embarrassed, teased, or shamed sexually. Someone might have done this to you directly or indirectly. What happened and how did you feel? How did you cope with the situation? When you think about the experience now, how do you feel?

Write about a time someone hurt you on purpose either emotionally or physically. What happened and how did you feel? How did you cope with this situation? When you think about the experience now, how do you feel?

Write about a time you were very upset about something and the people around you didn't seem to get it or care. What happened and how did you feel? How did you cope with the situation? When you think about the experience now, how do you feel?

How does reflecting on these experiences help you better understand your partner?

Putting It All Together

In this chapter, we discussed how sexual trauma survivors can heal in the context of a loving and secure relationship. We also reviewed ways you can take care of yourself while doing the important work of supporting your partner in their healing. You learned about mindful self-compassion, stress management skills, relationship boundaries, and building compassion and empathy as helpful ways to support both you and your partner. These skills can help you interrupt your painful relationship cycle and find new ways of approaching these moments of disconnection.

Reflect back on your relationship disconnection cycle that you explored in chapter 2. Take a moment to reflect on the pattern: what you tend to do, see your partner do, feel, and think when these moments of disconnection pop up.

Now, consider: when you reflect on your relationship disconnection cycle, how might you use mindful self-compassion to deescalate your emotions within the cycle? How might you speak to yourself compassionately about your feelings, remind yourself that what you are experiencing relates to the shared human experience, and mindfully notice your emotions that come up in this cycle in a balanced way?

When you reflect on your relationship disconnection cycle, how stressed do you think you feel in your body when this cycle comes up? How much do you think stress in your life increases your likelihood of being triggered into this cycle? And what do you tend to do after the disconnection cycle? Does the stress sit in your body and build, or do you find a way to release it? Is there an action you can take from the stress management and burnout avoidance strategies that may help you cope with the stress you feel in this cycle?

Also, are there any boundaries you or your partner are trying or wanting to communicate? Would it be helpful to broach the topic of boundaries with your partner so you can better support and understand each other in this cycle?

When you reflect on your relationship disconnection cycle, how much empathy do you have for what your partner is feeling in the moment? When we are triggered in our cycles, we often are focusing on our own emotions and trying to get our own needs met. What would it be like to instead try to increase your empathy and understanding for your partner's feelings? What would it be like to communicate this empathy to them?

Being a support person to a partner with sexual trauma is a lot of work. It can be exhausting, overwhelming, frustrating, and even scary at times. It is also incredibly rewarding to see your partner begin to relax more in the context of your relationship and the world, to see them feel safe in their body, and to experience connecting with each other on a deeper level. Healing does take time, though. There may be times that you feel powerless and struggle to keep providing support, wishing this trauma wasn't impacting them anymore. Know that your partner likely wishes this even more than you do, and if they could speed up their healing, they would. Patience is helpful as you take one step at a time. And remember to lean on your own self-care and stress management skills when these feelings come up, because you need support, too!

CHAPTER 4

Using Relationship Skills to Create a Secure Connection

Secure emotional intimacy—the ability to be close to one another and to feel safe with that person—is important for couples who are navigating the impact of sexual trauma on one or both partners. Sexual trauma can impact a person's ability to feel safe, trusting, understood, and supported. Being able to practice the capacities of active listening, empathy, and emotional attunement with an encouraging partner will promote healing. Ultimately, active listening, empathy, and emotional attunement help our partners feel safe with us so that they can open up—not just about their trauma, but also about their inner world. When we bond emotionally, our relationships become stronger. We also build a more secure attachment style, which, as we learned in chapter 1, is important within our relationship and also impacts how we feel about ourself.

This chapter will focus on teaching you effective communication skills and concepts that will better equip you to respond to and support your partner in conversation. These are tips I teach all the couples with whom I work (not only those working through sexual trauma), and ultimately, communication techniques like these can benefit all relationships and friendships. Your partner may be interested in these tips at some point as well. It's okay to ask them whether they would like to read this chapter if you think it might benefit them. Of course, when your partner's in a vulnerable place of healing, they might not be able to spend time focusing on learning better communication techniques, and it may feel one-sided to you as you practice your new skills to support them. That's okay too.

When you're in a conversation in which both people involved are hurting, you can practice going back and forth in the conversation with each person taking turns opening up as the other person listens. For the sake of this book, we are centering your partner's trauma experience and teaching you techniques to better support your partner and increase emotional connection in the relationship. But as your relationship strengthens, you might find your partner to be both more willing and more able to center your experience more of the time, and that both your partner and you benefit from using these skills in everyday communication.

In relationships, we take turns providing emotional support to each other; right now, it is your turn to provide the support. But to give you some hope, it's been rare that I've seen one partner commit to trying out supportive emotional communication skills without their partner noticing the positive impact and naturally starting to apply some of the skills in reciprocity.

Applying the valuable communication skills you'll learn in this chapter will enable your partner to
- have a safe place to open up about their trauma or triggers (if they want to);
- develop emotional trust and security in the context of your relationship, which can benefit their trauma healing as well as your relationship as a whole; and
- feel good being close to you—so you can feel good being close to them as well.

We'll begin with a crucial component of good communication: the ability to listen in order to truly understand.

Listening to Understand, Not to Respond

When you are sharing something that's important to you with someone else, can you tell the difference between when the other person is really listening and trying to understand you and when they are only partly listening while also preparing their response to you? Most of us feel better when someone is taking the first approach. When we can tell someone is understanding us (or at least trying to understand), we often feel more supported and more comfortable opening up.

When your partner opens up to you about how they are feeling, try to put your own thoughts on hold as you listen. This isn't about putting your own thoughts and feelings on hold forever, but more about hitting the pause button on those for now so you can better understand what your partner is sharing.

While this is a simple concept, it can be hard to apply in action. Why? Because our brain is working away during a conversation to help us decide what to say in response to someone—because we really want to be understood! Feeling understood is a human need. When both people are prioritizing their need to be understood at the same time, though, we often go around and around in circles without either one really understanding the other person. And right now, as you're helping them deal with their trauma, your partner's need to be understood is important. It's also one that you can afford to prioritize, more easily than they can yours.

Our first skill is to build the emotional muscle to pause our reactions, responses, opinions, and judgments. Letting it not be about us for a moment. There's nothing wrong with you if this is hard to do; with this as with any communication strategy, and any new behavior, patience is key.

Here are some ways you can practice listening to understand rather than to respond:

- Imagine an empty box. Now imagine storing your opinions, responses, and feelings about what your partner is sharing in this box. We're not locking these things away forever, but setting them aside for long enough to be fully present with what our partner is communicating. You might place your ideas about what your partner should do in this box, or even your fear that your partner will never feel better. *What are you going to place in your box?* Take a second to think or even journal about that now.
- Notice how it feels when your thoughts start to wander or something that your partner says makes your body start to feel a sensation that is just screaming, "STOP! I need to tell you what I think about that—I need to interrupt you right now because I think you might have something wrong." It would be very normal if this happens frequently in conversation (especially important conversations). Start to notice the signs in your brain or body that you want to turn the attention back to you—worry; a quickening heartbeat; an antsy, stressful feeling

that leaves you itching to interrupt; whatever it happens to be. It is okay that this happens because it's a natural response. You just want to become familiar with your own triggers, sensations, thoughts, and feelings so you can recognize them and slide them into that box you have next to you so you can return your attention to your partner. *What are some examples of thoughts or feelings that can make it hard to focus on what your partner is saying?*
- Use techniques to soothe yourself during the conversation so you can remain present. You might use deep breathing or something sensory like play dough or something to fidget with in your hands to decrease any anxiety you feel. *What helps you feel calm and focused?*
- As you listen to your partner, open your heart to what they are saying. Remind yourself that they are taking a risk in opening up about something important to them because they love you and hope you will understand them. Understand that feelings and perspectives aren't right or wrong, they just are. *Do you have a hard time believing this? Why or why not?*

Typically, conversations that aren't guided by this skill tend to have both partners entrenched in their respective positions, and in the pain or frustration they might be feeling, in a way that leaves each partner feeling misunderstood and angry or shut down. See the following dialogue, from *before* partner A learns the skill of listening to understand.

Partner A: What's wrong? I was just trying to give you a hug goodbye and you went stiff—are you mad at me?

Partner B: Mad at you? What? No, I had those nightmares again last night and I don't like being touched when I feel this way. I don't know—it's a lot.

Partner A: But that hurts my feelings—I was just trying to hug you. I'm not the one who hurt you, but you keep treating me like I am.

Now, here's an example of the same conversation *after* partner A has learned these skills.

Partner A: What's wrong? I was just trying to give you a hug goodbye and you went stiff—are you mad at me?

Partner B: Mad at you? What? No, I had those nightmares again last night and I don't like being touched when I feel this way. I don't know—it's a lot.

Partner A: (notices their feelings are hurt by what Partner B is saying, but takes a deep breath and puts their reactions in the pause box for now) Oh, wow, that does sound like a lot. Do you want to talk about it?

Partner B: Yeah, I guess I do ... I mean, I feel bad that you felt me go stiff—I don't want to hurt you. But I'm sensitive in the mornings after the nightmares because the images of what happened to me keep playing in my mind. And, like, I know you're a safe person, but my body doesn't trust it because my mind is stuck replaying those terrible things.

In this scenario, partner B feels better opening up about this sensitive topic, and they're relieved that partner A is trying to understand.

Mirroring and Empathy

Mirroring is my favorite communication skill to teach. It is one of the best ways to develop a sense of empathy for another person and to convey your presence and empathy to them.

What is mirroring? Mirroring is when you reflect back what your partner is sharing with you, in a genuine and non-mocking way. When you mirror in conversation, you might use the same words your partner is saying, or you might summarize or highlight the most important parts of what they said, as you heard them, and check back with them to see whether you understood what they really meant.

The magic in mirroring is that when we speak our partner's words, we start feeling empathy, in our minds and our bodies, as we imagine ourselves in our partner's shoes. When we feel empathy, our bodies become less defensive or reactive. We are less likely to take things personally, less likely to feel anger toward that person or to feel attacked by that person. When our partner feels our empathy, they also become less defensive. They feel a sense of calm as they feel our presence, attention, and understanding.

Here are some specific ways to practice mirroring and empathy.

- Reflect back to your partner what they are saying using either their words or your own as you summarize or highlight the most important parts.
- Pay attention to how your partner responds when you do this. Some people don't like when you use their exact same words because it might feel robotic to them or mocking, but some really like you to use their exact words because it shows you really get it—they might share this with you or you can ask.

- Imagine yourself in your partner's shoes as you mirror back what they are sharing with you. How might they be feeling or what might they be thinking?
- Notice how your partner may open up even more or on a deeper level when you use mirroring in conversation.
- Notice how your own perspectives shift or you start to understand things differently as you really sit in your partner's experience.
- If your partner doesn't use feeling words or share how they are feeling directly, but you think you might have an idea, you can make a conjecture. If they correct you, that's okay—your guess was still helpful because it allows them to open up more. If it seems like you got the feeling word right, your partner might feel really close to you as you show them you understand.

Here, picking up from where the previous conversation left off, is an example of a conversation as it might take place *before* partner A has learned the skill of mirroring and empathy. As a reminder, Partner A's last comment was: "But that hurts my feelings—I was just trying to hug you. I'm not the one who hurt you, but you keep treating me like I am."

Partner B: Yeah, I guess I do ... I mean, I feel bad that you felt me go stiff—I don't want to hurt you. But I'm sensitive in the mornings after the nightmares because the images of what happened to me keep playing in my mind. And, like, I know you're a safe person, but my body doesn't trust it because my mind is stuck replaying those terrible things.

Partner A: Wow, thank you for sharing.

The conversation ends just as partner B starts opening up about something important.

By contrast, if partner A knows how to practice mirroring and empathy, they might be able to bring the conversation further and give their partner more opportunities to be open and to heal. Again, partner B is picking up where we left off.

Partner B: Yeah, I guess I do ... I mean, I feel bad that you felt me go stiff—I don't want to hurt you. But I'm sensitive in the mornings after the nightmares because the images of what happened to me keep playing in my mind. And, like, I know you're a safe person, but my body doesn't trust it because my mind is stuck replaying those terrible things.

Partner A: (practicing the mirroring skill) Oh wow, you're still feeling like you're in that nightmare right now. It was like it wasn't me reaching to hug you, but someone scary.

Partner B: (feeling very understood now, so they open up even more) Yes, exactly. Part of me is still back there in that nightmare—well, really in the assault. I just froze when you touched me because it was startling. Like someone grabbed me. And I just freeze, and my heart pounds.

Partner A: (mirroring again to show they get it and have empathy for partner B) So even though you are here with me, it's like your body and your mind are still back there at the assault. And when I touched you, it startled you. That sounds really scary.

Partner B: (feeling close to Partner A now as they feel even more understood) Yes, so scary. And then I feel bad because I do really like hugs from you. I don't want you to stop hugging me. But I also really don't want to be so scared.

EXERCISE: Practicing Mirroring and Empathy

Read through each of the examples below, and either think about or journal what you would say in response if your goal is to mirror and empathize with what you're hearing.

1. The other day when I was leaving my therapy session, I felt so tired. We weren't

even talking about my trauma that much, but I felt so drained.
2. When I made the report to the police, it was overwhelming because I was still in a brain fog and I had to answer so many questions.
3. It's really hard to go to work every day when that is where it happened.

Validation

Validating our partners when they open up can have the biggest impact of anything we say in our communication. One of the hardest parts about emotional suffering is feeling like no one understands how bad it hurts or fearing that others are judging us. Many of us feel this in even day-to-day common hurts. When our partner has experienced sexual trauma, they likely have been invalidated by many people. Each time someone questions the reality of what happened, or their perpetrator states that it was a consensual event or even denies it happened, or they are treated like they've lost their mind when they have symptoms of PTSD, it can push someone away from feeling like anyone will ever understand them.

But when we know how to validate our partner about how they are feeling, they begin to feel less alone. They can relax into us and know that they are safe with us. They can feel believed, understood, and supported.

Here are some tips for practicing validation.

- When you are listening to your partner, practicing putting yourself in their shoes, and imagining how they may feel, consider everything you know to be true about your partner and how what they are feeling makes sense to you. Keep in mind that someone's feelings can make sense to you even if their opinions or beliefs do not. Say your partner comes home one night feeling like their boss was judgmental to them at work. When you hear the story, you might disagree about whether their boss was actually being judgmental toward them. But the fact remains that your partner's hurting, so it's your job to try to understand that pain and to validate it as something that's okay to feel, even if you also try to talk to your partner about the context and what you think might have happened. If your partner has been judged repeatedly by others, for example after pressing charges against their perpetrator, they are likely feeling ganged up on and vulnerable. If someone says something to them that you don't think was intended to be judgmental, it can still make sense to you that your partner was hurt by it. That is what you want to

communicate to your partner—that their feelings make sense.
- A simple and effective way to validate is to lead with "That makes sense to me because..."
- If your partner's feelings don't make sense to you, that is just a hint that there is more to understand. They may have not shared everything yet, or you may just not be able to understand where they're coming from yet. In these moments, you can keep using mirroring and empathy to help them open up, or you can use open-ended questions, which will be the next strategy we discuss.

Here's an example of a conversation *before* partner A learns validation (picking up from where we left off before).

Partner B: Yes, so scary. And then I feel bad because I do really like hugs from you. I don't want you to stop hugging me. But I also really don't want to be so scared.

Partner A: (trying to convince Partner B that they don't need to feel this way) I still don't understand, though, why you can't just calm down, when all you have to do is look at me to know it's me. I'm not a scary person, so just remind yourself it's me and you won't feel scared.

Here you'll see that partner A has jumped to looking at the situation from *their* own perspective, not their partner's. They're also leaping to give advice that might be really difficult for their partner to actually implement. After all, most of us can understand in the abstract that, say, our partner isn't a scary person and doesn't intend to harm us. It's the experience of trauma, and the vividness of it, that can make it difficult for us to actually *feel* that this is true, until we process and heal our trauma.

Here's how partner A responds after learning the skill of validation.

Partner B: Yes, so scary. And then I feel bad because I do really like hugs from you. I don't want you to stop hugging me. But I also really don't want to be so scared.

Partner A: (practicing the validation skill) That sounds so confusing for you. It makes sense to me that you are scared by my touch when you're still feeling shaken up by your nightmare. Nightmares can feel so real sometimes.

EXERCISE: *Practicing Validation*

Think about a time when you felt really understood by someone. How did they show you that you were important to them? How did they convey that they were listening? And how did you feel after the interaction?

You might journal about your responses to these questions, if you like. And really try to let yourself sit with how meaningful this memory of being validated and understood is to you and the gift it is that someone treated you this way. Then, consider: what are some ways you can give your partner this same experience of being recognized and understood?

Now, let's try some validation. Read through each of the examples below, and either think about or journal what you would say in response if your goal is to validate your partner's experience. You might start your validation response with the phrase, "That makes sense to me because..."

1. Today I had a flashback in my therapy session; I felt scared and worried that I wouldn't be able to calm down.
2. Someone at work kept pressing me about why I switched departments. They don't know about the assault, and I felt so frustrated that they kept pressing me for more details about why I made the transfer.
3. I want to start running again, but every time I get dressed to head out, I can't bring myself to get out there alone on the road again.

Open-Ended Questions

When you are having trouble understanding your partner, you can ask open-ended questions to help them open up. You always want to make sure that your partner is comfortable with you asking them questions. If they are not ready to open up yet and you come at them with a lot of questions, they may feel pressured or like they are being interrogated.

Here are some tips for asking open-ended questions:

- Lead with something like "I really love when you share more about how you are feeling because I learn more about you that helps me know how to support and love you. Is it okay if I ask you a question? It's okay if you don't want me to or end up not wanting to answer it."
- Try to ask only one or two open-ended questions per conversation.
- As your partner opens up, use all the skills you've learned so far—listening to understand (not to respond), mirroring and empathizing, validating—to ensure they continue to feel supported in the conversation.
- Thank them for sharing their thoughts and feelings with you.

Here's what it looks like when partner A uses open-ended questions.

Partner A: That sounds so confusing for you. It makes sense to me that you are scared by my touch when you're still feeling shaken up by your nightmare. Nightmares can feel so real sometimes.

Partner B: Yeah, so real.

Partner A: (asking for consent before asking Partner B the question) Now that I'm understanding better how you are feeling, is it okay if I ask you a question about it?

Partner B: Yes, but I'm worried about what you are going to ask me. Sometimes I don't know the answer when people ask me questions about this stuff.

Partner A: (practicing the validation skill and giving permission to Partner B to set a boundary) That's okay. It makes sense to me that you're worried. How about, I ask the question and if for whatever reason you don't want to talk about it, that's okay? You can answer now or later, or even not at all if you don't want.

Partner B: Okay. What is it?

Partner A: (asking an open-ended question) When you feel this way after nightmares, what can I do to help?

Partner B: Oh—it's kind of you to ask. I don't know if there's anything you can do, actually. The feeling just stays with me for some time. My therapist said it's normal, and we're working on trying some things in therapy to help decrease the nightmares, but there's not a lot I can do to make the bad feeling go away—it kinda stays with me for a couple of hours.

Partner A: (validating) Oh, I see. That makes sense, that the feeling just stays around, because I know you've told me how your nightmares can feel so real.

Partner B: Yeah. I don't know. Maybe I could let you know when I wake up if I've had a nightmare the night before? Then on those mornings, if you could ask me if there's anything I need? And maybe you can ask before hugging me those mornings just so I can let you know whether I'm in the mood or not?

Partner A: Yes, I think that's a great idea.

You'll see that asking open-ended questions, and employing skills like mirroring and validation, have helped these partners explore a potential site of conflict together in a kind and empathic manner—where otherwise each of them might have been stuck in their own pain, fighting to get their own needs met in a way that makes it difficult to reach any resolution.

Nonverbal Communication

We all can feel supported when someone shows us positive nonverbal communication techniques. But nonverbal cues can be especially important to people with trauma because of the hypervigilance and increased awareness of the environment and the people around them that they experience.

Here are some examples of nonverbal communication that may be helpful:
- Facing your partner (unless they ask that you not look at them while they talk)
- Having a calm demeanor
- Keeping a relaxed posture and uncrossed arms
- Keeping a neutral facial expression or matching your partner's emotional presence (example: they are telling you something sad, they look sad, and your facial expression is also sad to show concern)
- Nodding your head or making encouraging sounds as they share

- Not towering above your partner; if they are seated, sitting at their level
- If your partner likes physical touch as reassurance: holding their hand, rubbing their back, or giving them a hug. Of course, because of their trauma, your partner may not respond the same way at all times when it comes to physical touch, so it might be helpful to ask them whether the touch is okay before you reach out.

Some Advice About Advice

Humans like to give each other advice. And sometimes advice is very helpful, especially when we are in pain and we don't know what to do. Here's the other thing about humans: we also don't like being told what to do.

We humans can be very confusing.

You are likely someone who finds advice helpful sometimes. How do I know that? You are reading a self-help book filled with advice. What is different about you in this moment than your partner is that you chose to read this book because you were ready for the advice. Your partner might not be looking for advice from you (or anyone) at this stage of their healing.

Sometimes people want advice, but other times people want to vent or just want to be understood. Sometimes that is all they need to feel better and there really isn't anything more you need to do.

Giving people advice when what they are looking for is empathy can lead to tension and misunderstandings. When one person in a conversation just had the intention to help, but the other doesn't feel helped at all and actually feels even more misunderstood, it ends up hurting both people in the conversation—especially when the advice giver feels hurt or rejected that the person receiving the advice didn't want it. So complicated!

Here's the magic solution: always ask before you provide your partner with advice. This is helpful in just about any interaction. Unless someone explicitly asks for advice, ask them whether they want advice before you provide any.

When you're in conversations with your partner where you see an opportunity to give them advice or your opinion on how they might handle something, you might say, "Wow, thank you for sharing this with me. It sounds like so much to deal with! When you are feeling this way, would you like my opinions or advice, or would you prefer that I listen and support only? I'm okay either way—I know we need different types of support at different times." Or, if in the course of a conversation you find yourself itching to tell your partner how you think they should handle a given situation, try to put that reaction in the pause box and understand and validate what they tell you instead.

What to Do When You Get It Wrong

I want to acknowledge that when you're doing your best to understand your partner and express empathy and support for them, you are being vulnerable and taking a risk. It's not easy to try to open space for someone to respond to emotions and experiences that may be quite difficult for them to navigate. And you may feel sensitive, too. So, when we get something wrong in our partner's eyes (and we will because we are human and communication is never perfect), we may feel criticized or attacked right when we're trying our best to be helpful. That can really hurt.

It can be helpful to understand that when your partner corrects you or tells you that you are not understanding them, it's coming from a place of hurt—and a place of really needing to feel close to you. Feeling understood by you is what they are most hoping for because when they feel understood by someone they love, they feel less alone with their pain.

It's okay to feel hurt by their correction, and also know that the correction is just another opportunity to be close to them and understand them better. The patience you show your partner during these moments, and your willingness to put hurt feelings to one side, can pay off immensely in the trust and closeness you will feel as you and your partner navigate these situations together. It also opens up the space for you to use a productive communication strategy next—listening to the correction, acknowledging what your partner's telling you about what they feel and what you did wrong, making your intentions clear without invalidating them, and making amends or changes in your behavior in whatever way is most appropriate for the situation.

Practicing Communication Skills

You might choose to practice these new skills through your normal interactions with your partner, doing your best to incorporate the strategies into your conversations and interactions organically. You may decide to let your partner know that you are reading this book and that they might notice you are working on your communication skills to better support them.

If your partner is open to it, consider using some of the conversation prompts below to open up deeper conversations. And make sure you receive consent from your partner.

Here are some good guidelines if you use these prompts:
- Let your partner know what you have learned in this chapter. Ask them whether they would

be open to increasing emotional connection through guided conversation prompts.
- Decide together on a good place and time for the conversations. It is helpful to have more intimate conversations when you are in a place where you can feel calm, away from distractions, and comfortable opening up to each other.
- Allow either partner to veto a conversation topic if they are uncomfortable or not ready to talk about that particular topic.
- Some of these prompts are directly related to the impact of the trauma on your partner, yourself, or the relationship. Some of these prompts are more generally related to relationships and emotional connection. Allow your partner to decide whether they would like to discuss the trauma-related prompts or the more general ones. Both are helpful—and the trauma-related prompts may be more triggering.
- Remember that the goal of the conversations is to learn more about each other and bring you closer. It's okay to take a pause if the conversations become too overwhelming for either of you. You can return later or offer the other understanding.
- We bond in small moments—there is no need to spend hours discussing these prompts. You

might spend twenty minutes, you might spend forty-five minutes. Either way, set a game plan with each other so neither person feels pressured to talk all night long. And limit the conversation to one or two prompts in a sitting.

Below you'll find a list of prompts to help with emotional bonding followed by prompts related to sexual trauma. You can also find a worksheet with these prompts on the book's website, http://www.newharbinger.com/51574. Look over the lists and see which feel like they might be helpful to you and your partner for initiating a conversation. And again, remember to get your partner's consent first. remember to get your partner's consent first.

> ### PROMPTS RELATED TO EMOTIONAL BONDING
>
> *Each of us has needs when we are hurting. Some of us need connection, some of us want to be alone, some of us might want help distracting ourselves from the pain. What kind of support do you like in different times of hurting?*
>
> *People show love in different ways. A mother might rub her child's back when they aren't feeling well, a friend might drop off flowers on a birthday, a partner might like to plan special dates to celebrate special occasions. How do you like to*

be shown love? Are there any ways that people show you love that make you uncomfortable?

When we need support, we let that be known in different ways. Some of us might ask directly for a hug, some might text a friend to check in, some keep it to themselves, or some might pick a fight without even realizing it. When you need support, how do you let that be known?

How did the adults in your childhood show you love and attention? How did they disappoint you? What did you need from those adults to help you feel more loved, understood, and valued?

What signs show you that your partner is present with you, and what signs show you that they are distracted? How does it feel to you when they are present, and how does it feel to you when they are distracted? (Refrain from giving criticism; this is to help your partner understand how you experience them so they can adapt when you really need them.)

Share a memory of when you felt most connected to your partner. Share all the details you remember from the memory and how it felt.

Share a memory of when you felt great joy in your life. Share all the details you remember from the memory, how it felt, and what it means to you.

Share a memory of when you felt great sadness in your life. How was that experience for you, what did you learn, and was anyone there to support you?

PROMPTS RELATED TO SEXUAL TRAUMA

Do you have any trauma triggers that I don't know about but you would like to share with me? How can I support you if you are triggered?

Is there anything related to how you've been feeling about the impact of the trauma that you haven't told me but want to share with me? It is okay to let me know how you would like me to support you as you share.

Do you have any fears related to our relationship and how the sexual trauma has impacted either you, me, or our relationship generally?

Is there anything you would like me to start doing or stop doing to help support your trauma healing?

When it's all too much, what is the best outlet to distract you from pain, and how can I support you with this?

When you need support facing the tough stuff, is there anything I can do to help you feel less alone?

Putting It All Together

The communication skills you learned in this chapter can help build a deep trust and understanding in your relationship. It is possible to feel trust and connection without practicing these skills, but when you discuss vulnerable or distressing topics, it's much more likely that your communication can go off the rails, leaving you both feeling hurt and misunderstood. Helping your partner share their inner world, fears, and desires with you in a safe way can build a secure attachment in your relationship and open the door to the type of love and connection we all crave.

These relationship skills can be easier to practice when one or both partners are coming from a place of calm. But what happens when one or both of you are in a great deal of distress? We will build upon these tools in the next chapter, which focuses on coping with trauma triggers.

CHAPTER 5
Coping with Trauma Triggers

When your partner is triggered, they may seem scared, angry, panicked, shut down, or terrified. They might be communicative to you, or unable to speak. It might seem like whatever you do to help isn't working—you might not even be aware of what triggered them in the first place. You might get so overwhelmed yourself that it seems like your reaction to them makes things worse.

When someone with sexual trauma is triggered, their mind and body react very fast—so fast, it can be hard for your partner or anyone around them to understand what exactly happened. Once their reaction has passed and your partner seems like their normal self, it can be tempting to not reflect on the distressing moment out of fear that you'll trigger your partner (or yourself) again. But by avoiding a discussion of what happened, you might miss out on learning new ways to support your partner when moments like these occur in the future.

It is just so hard to feel helpless when our partner is in pain. We get stuck in a pain of our own. Let's learn more about these moments and how to move through them in ways that build more trust and security in your relationship. This will not only help your partner with their trauma healing, but it can also improve your relationship overall as each of you begins to see the other person as someone who is there for you even in the most distressing moments.

In this chapter you will learn about the science of what is going on in your partner's body when they are triggered, how to slow down and regulate the overwhelming response that happens to both of you in these moments, and how to come back together to repair any hurts that happened in moments when you were both too triggered to find connection.

Common Triggers

A *trigger* is anything that activates your partner to experience their trauma or PTSD symptoms. Each person is different in what specifically can trigger their trauma response. In this section, we'll discuss common triggers for sexual trauma survivors. I'll also include discussion prompts that you and your partner can use to learn more about their triggers.

Sexual trauma survivors may be triggered by anything that reminds them of their traumatic experiences. Triggers may be things that your partner may see, touch or feel, hear, taste, or smell that brings them back to their traumatic memory. Your partner may or may not be fully aware of their triggers. Sometimes their reaction to the trigger is so fast and overwhelming that they aren't able to know what it was that triggered them. They may or may not be ready to slow down and explore their triggers yet, so it's important to take their lead in how much they want to or can communicate to you about their triggers and trauma response.

Below I've compiled a noncomprehensive list of sexual trauma triggers a person may experience. If you are a survivor of sexual or relationship trauma yourself, reading this list may feel overwhelming or trigger you. It's okay to skip this section or take pauses as you read to soothe yourself.

- Seeing, interacting with, hearing about, or otherwise being reminded of an abuser
- Visiting or being reminded of the location of the abuse
- Seeing an object that reminds them of something they noticed or focused on during the abuse
- Being in situations that remind them of the abuse or the times or experiences around the time of their life that the abuse took place
- Being asked about or interrogated about the abuse
- Being touched in ways that remind them of specific memories of the abuse

- Seeing sexual content or abuse in the media (television, film, theater, news, books, magazines, music, artwork)
- Being in situations that make them feel trapped, powerless, controlled, or vulnerable
- Experiencing people and places that remind them of their life at the time of the abuse
- Interacting with other people who are the same age as they were during the abuse
- Being told a story of someone else's sexual trauma
- Smelling a scent that is connected to their memories of the abuse
- Tasting something that reminds them of the abuse
- Having sex or other physically intimate experiences
- Seeing a piece of clothing from the time of the abuse
- Anniversaries—the time of year around the traumatic experiences or significant dates (for example, when it started or stopped)

Trauma Responses

When your partner is triggered, they may have a trauma response. Our bodies are wired to help us survive threatening situations. When we face a situation that threatens our physical or emotional safety, our body quickly goes into protection mode; our sympathetic nervous system, which controls the bodily systems that help us respond to danger, is activated to help us face the stressful event.

Signs our sympathetic nervous system is activated include the following:
- Our pupils enlarge to improve our vision.
- Our heart rate increases to improve the flow of oxygen throughout our bodies.
- Our airway muscles relax to improve the flow of oxygen to our lungs.
- We shake or tremble as our muscles prepare for action.
- Our reflexes, endurance, and strength are improved.
- Our digestive system slows so energy can be used in other parts of our body.

This nervous system response is meant to happen for short periods of time to help us survive life-threatening events. Experiences of sexual trauma, however, can be stored in the body, keeping us stuck. When we experience something that reminds us of the trauma, we can be triggered back to the experience as if we are back in the threatening situation. And when we're triggered, it's like our body and mind are re-experiencing the trauma and it's hard to stay present in the current moment and connect to those around us.

You've probably heard of the sympathetic nervous system response commonly referred to as the fight-or-flight response, and you've possibly heard of the longer term fight-flight-freeze response. More recently, a fourth component—fawn—has been added (Walker 2013). Let's break down these four common trauma responses; you may recognize your partner and yourself in the descriptions.

Fight

In a fight response, we may express anger or become bigger in our emotions and body language to protect ourselves from the perceived threat. Our reaction may be saying, "Stay away from me if you want to be safe! Do not threaten me!" If your partner is triggered to a fight response, you may notice that they:
- express anger
- use body language or facial expressions to intimidate, attack, or push others away
- criticize, complain
- initiate arguments or snap back in defensiveness

Flight

In a flight response, we may want to remove ourselves from perceived threats as quickly as possible or avoid them altogether. We may have an automatic urge to remove ourselves from a situation or trigger because it feels too anxiety provoking to engage with the trigger or to

function with the trigger in the environment. If your partner is triggered to a flight response, you may notice that they:
- leave situations or isolate when triggered
- turn attention to other activities (like work) to distract themselves
- appear scared or anxious
- avoid conflict or triggers

Freeze

In a freeze response, we may appear physically present but emotionally or mentally checked out. We may dissociate, or we may use numbing behaviors to escape the perceived threat. If your partner is triggered to a freeze response, you may notice that they:
- become dissociative, shutdown, or unresponsive
- rely on numbing behaviors like substance abuse, disordered eating, or gambling
- spend an excessive amount of time watching TV or scrolling on social media
- seem stuck or not there; may appear scared or may seem unemotional

Fawn

In a fawn response, we attempt to make ourselves safe by staying likable and engaging in people-pleasing actions. We may shrink or hide our feelings of anger or fear so as not to trigger those around us. We may feel the only way to keep ourselves safe is to keep everyone around us happy. If your partner is triggered to a fawn response, you may notice that they:

- people-please or put others' needs before their own
- appear to go into helper or fix-it mode when triggered
- seem like everything is okay even if it isn't
- eventually burn out and become resentful

EXERCISE: Identifying Triggers and Trauma Responses

Now that you have some foundational understanding of how triggers and trauma responses impact your partner, you can invite your partner to share their experience of these things with you. Remember that your partner may or may not be ready to discuss these topics with you; if they show nervousness about having these conversations, don't pressure them to open up until they are ready. You can let them know that you're learning more about this topic and how to help them, and you'll be there if and when they want to share more about their experience with you.

The following are reflection and discussion prompts. If you two are discussing this together, you may notice that talking through these prompts builds more understanding and connection. Your partner may only be able to discuss one or two prompts at a time; support them in any boundaries they set. And if your partner isn't ready to have these discussions, you can self-reflect on your own experiences and observations of your partner. (An "Identifying Triggers and Trauma Responses" worksheet is available at http://www.newharbinger.com/51574, if you feel it'll be helpful.)

- Do you know some of your triggers, and are there any you want to share with me?
- Is there anything I do that triggers you? What is it like for you when that happens?
- Do you identify with any of the trauma responses (fight, flight, freeze, or fawn)? What is it like for you when you go into your trauma response?
- How does it feel in your body when you are triggered?
- What urges do you have when you are triggered?
- What thoughts do you have when you are triggered?
- What feelings do you have when you are triggered?
- What kind of support do you need from me when you are triggered into a trauma response?

When you know about your partner's triggers and their trauma response, you can get better at supporting them. When your partner is in fight, flight, freeze, or fawn mode, it might be hard for them to connect with you authentically and you may become triggered yourself. We'll talk more about this, and what you can do if that happens, shortly.

Coregulation

Coregulation is a term used to describe when a person is able to help another person, in a calm and supportive way, to move through their trauma response and find their way to a more regulated space. Relationship attachment science has shown that coregulation can be more effective than self-soothing skills when someone has a trauma trigger.

Just as you can support your partner in conflict by staying present and using the communication skills we've discussed in this book, you can support your partner when they are having a trauma response by helping them access safety in their connection with you.

The goal of offering your partner coregulation, using the strategies you'll learn in this section, is not to control or change their emotions. Their emotions and their trauma response is normal. Always reassure them that their emotions and reactions are normal, and give them choices when it comes to how you might respond or what the two of you might do next—they may want your help or not, and that is okay.

You might also share this chapter of the book with your partner, when they are not triggered or overwhelmed, and get their feedback. They can let you know which trauma response they believe they tend to have and what coregulation help they are open to accepting.

Below are coregulation strategies you can use for the four different nervous system responses: fight, flight, freeze, and fawn.

Coregulating a Fight Response

- Stay present with your partner; acknowledge their feelings of anger and rage; let them know it makes sense that they are having this reaction.
- Try not to shut down or "get big" in response to them, with dramatic and forceful emotions, even if you really do feel agitated by what you are seeing or hearing. Know that under their anger, your partner is scared, and it's easy for them to feel rejected or abandoned.
- Use the mirroring, empathy, and validation skills you learned in chapter 4.
- Let your partner know that anger is okay and healthy, and that you don't think they need

to change how they feel. Reassure them that if they do want help grounding themself, you are there to support them.
- If their anger becomes emotionally or physically dangerous, set boundaries. Example: "I can see you are upset and it makes sense to me that you would be. I love you and I want to support you. When you (describe what they are doing), I get scared and don't know how to support you. If you can stay in conversation with me without (e.g., calling me names, threatening me, hurting yourself), I will stay to support you." If they're not able to do what you're asking them to, take a time-out.

Coregulating a Flight Response

- Reassure your partner that it's okay for them to take space and time-outs when they are overwhelmed.
- Calmly and reassuringly ask your partner what they need from you; it's okay if they don't know. "I can stay close or give you space." "I don't need to say anything if you want me to stay with you; we can just breathe together and be."
- Encourage your partner to come back to you when they want to talk; reassure them that

you care and even if their feelings or thoughts don't make 100% sense to them, you are there to hear them.
- Help them cope with stress and burnout using the stress management skills in chapter 3.

Coregulating a Freeze Response

- In a calm, steady voice, let your partner know that you see them freezing or shutting down and that it's okay that they do that when they are overwhelmed.
- Ask them whether they would like to take some deep breaths with you.
- Reassure them that even when they freeze like this, you are here with them when they need you.
- Ask them whether they'd like you to stay with them or to give them space. If they ask for space, let them know they can come to you for connection at any time. Let them know when you will check in with them.
- Help them utilize anything that helps them feel safe, such as a weighted blanket, using senses to ground themselves, or meditation and breathing exercises.

Coregulating a Fawn Response

- Reassure your partner that it's okay for them to be human and imperfect.
- Help your partner say no to overwhelming activities or set boundaries if needed.
- Ask your partner whether they want to talk about their feelings; reassure them they are not a burden and that their feelings make sense.
- Limit criticism or feedback.
- Help them cope with stress and burnout using the stress management skills in chapter 3.

When You're Triggered

Offering coregulation to your partner can be hard because you may become triggered yourself. In secure relationships, you are able to take turns stepping into coregulation, and you might even practice your coregulation skills at the same time. But if your partner is having a trauma response themselves, and grappling with sexual trauma generally, it is harder for them to share the coregulation responsibility. If your partner is not able to coregulate because of their trauma responses, you can use self-soothing techniques as you offer them coregulation.

In this section, I provide tips for self-soothing depending on which response you have. First, it's helpful to know that certain responses are more likely to occur depending on what your attachment style is. If you need a refresher on attachment styles, refer back to the section on attachment theory in chapter 1. A *fight* response or *fawn* response tends to occur when someone with an anxious or disorganized attachment style is triggered in the relationship. A *flight* response or *freeze* response tends to occur when someone with an avoidant or disorganized attachment style is triggered in the relationship.

If you have any of these responses when you are triggered, you can soothe yourself in the following ways:
- Start noticing how it feels in your body when you are triggered. What do you notice happening when you start to become triggered?
- Use breathing and soothing techniques to help you feel calm.
- If you cannot soothe yourself enough to stay present and use your communication skills, ask for a pause or time-out. Reassure your partner that you want to discuss it again when you are not feeling so overwhelmed.

Here's where your different responses might come into play:
- If you have a *fight* response, instead of criticizing, attacking, or defending, use I-statements to share your feelings and thoughts.

- If you have a *flight* response, instead of defending yourself, changing the subject, or minimizing your partner's feelings, use mirroring, empathy, and validation in response to what your partner is sharing.
- To soothe a *freeze* response, instead of going silent as you go numb, dissociate, or criticize yourself in your mind, use mirroring, empathy, and validation in response to what your partner is sharing.
- Finally, to soothe a *fawn* response, instead of trying to fix the situation, rescuing your partner, giving suggestions or feedback, or flattering your partner, use I-statements to share your feelings and thoughts.

Even with all the love you have for your partner, and all the effort you both are putting in to try to stay connected and loving during times of distress, there are always going to be times that you hurt each other and things just don't go very well. When you are triggered and overstimulated, you may say things you don't mean, dismiss your partner's feelings, or shut down completely, leaving your partner feeling abandoned.

What do you do when this happens?

Many relationship experts agree that it's important to repair these moments by coming together after you are no longer overwhelmed so that you can make sense of what happened, understand both your own and your partner's reaction, and show compassion for your partner and your impact on them.

I'm going to outline some ways you can repair these moments. Know, though, that these moments aren't going to be perfect and your repair attempts may feel awkward at first. It might even seem like your efforts aren't working. Just showing up and trying shows your partner you care, though, and you will get better at these attempts the more you try.

Taking a Time-Out

Deciding to take a pause from an argument or stressful situation when we are overstimulated can help lay the groundwork for a successful relationship repair. Often our bodies are signaling that we need to walk away from an overwhelming situation in order to have the space we need to feel grounded and safe again. Just as our fight-flight-freeze-fawn responses can be related to our attachment style, so can the way we handle these signals that a time-out may be needed.

If you have an anxious attachment style, you may push through these signals and stay in a discussion long past the time it's productive because you're scared that you won't be able to find resolution and connection with your partner if you pause the conversation. This can increase your partner's overwhelm when what they need is space to soothe themselves.

If you have an avoidant attachment style, you may shut down the moment you start getting these signals. Even if you don't physically walk away from the discussion, outwardly you may be noncommunicative. This can increase your partner's overwhelm when they need reassurance that finding resolution and connection with them is important to you.

If you have a disorganized attachment style, depending on the situation, you may either push the conversation or shut down. You and your partner may have a hard time predicting your reaction, which can increase the overwhelm you both feel in these moments.

If you have a secure attachment style, you are more likely to be aware of both your and your partner's needs and signals. This can help you self-soothe while also providing support to your partner. No one is able to do this 100% of the time, but you generally can stay calm and connected in times of distress, which can help you and your partner coregulate.

Sometimes it's too hard to stay in conversation without escalating all your triggered anxious, avoidant, or disorganized attachment behaviors that can hurt your partner. In these moments, you can move toward a more secure attachment style by reassuring your partner that you want to return to your discussion after you both feel more soothed. The next exercise will give you a road map for doing this.

EXERCISE: Making a Time-Out Agreement

You can move toward a more secure attachment style in your relationship by making an agreement with your partner about what you will do in these moments of overwhelm. This exercise will walk you through making this agreement. You'll want to invite your partner into this activity so you can make an agreement that works well for both of you.

You might want to keep a notebook nearby as you work through these questions together. Or you can use the worksheet that's available at http://www.newharbinger.com/51574. Make notes on what you agree on because you can return to this agreement in the future. It's also normal to notice as time goes by that you need to make adjustments to the agreement if some parts just aren't working out as planned.

What do we do or say when we need a time-out?

You might come up with a code word or phrase to let your partner know when you need to take a pause in your discussion. Think back to a time when you were in an overwhelming moment with your partner and you both would have benefited from taking a pause on the topic in order to come back to a more grounded place. If your partner initiated the pause, how would you have liked them to do that?

Some examples could be:
- A vulnerable ask. "I am feeling overwhelmed and I'm afraid we will keep hurting each other more if we go on like this. I want to come back to this talk when I am calmer. Can we take a pause?"
- Using a code word like "pineapple." "This feels like a pineapple situation. Let's pause and come back later."
- Short and direct: "I need a pause to calm down. Can we take a time-out?"

Discuss this with your partner and write down how you would like to initiate a time-out with your partner. Also remember, you might not get it exactly right in the moment, and that's okay, but having a plan empowers you to start trying something new even if it's imperfect.

Is there anything each of us wants the other to know when we take a timeout, even if we can't say it directly when we are overwhelmed?

You or your partner may feel rejected or abandoned when the other person asks for a time-out. Is there anything you need to hear or know in these moments? You might need to hear or remember that your partner loves you and that you are important to them. You may need reassurance that they are taking the space so they can be a better partner when they come back.

Reflect on this and write down what each partner needs to hear or not. Practice saying these things to each other. You might be able to say this in the moment before taking the pause. If you are too overwhelmed, you might not be able to, so it's important for your partner to be able to turn back to this agreement and remember that these words are true even if you don't say them aloud in the moment.

How long will our time-out last?

Different situations call for different amounts of time. If you're the partner to ask for the time-out, let your partner know when you think you'll be ready to return to the discussion. It could be that you think you'll be ready in less than an hour after you get some space. Or maybe you know that it's going to take more time. Ultimately, you should feel safe to ask for the time you need. If you take longer than a day to come back to the discussion, though, it can send the message to your partner that you're avoiding the conversation, even if you have the best of intentions—so, make sure you take that reality into account as you're setting parameters for your time-outs.

How will you let each other know how long you'll need? Write this down in your notebook.

How will we soothe ourselves during our time-out?

What helps you soothe yourself when you are overwhelmed and triggered? You might want to refer back to the sections in chapter 3 on mindful self-compassion and stress management and show these sections to your partner if they haven't seen them and you think it might be helpful.

When you are triggered, your brain can get stuck focusing on thoughts and feelings that keep you stuck. That's why it's important to do something that helps you transition away from your stuck thoughts and feelings before you come back to each other.

How will you soothe yourselves in these moments? Each of you can write down a few ideas that come to mind.

What do we do when we return to this discussion after the time-out?

You might interact with each other before you are able to discuss what happened in your triggered states. It's important that you respect any boundaries that either of you asked for and not initiate discussion of the triggered moments until both of you are ready to do so. When you do return to each other to better understand what happened, make sure you are away from distractions and can tune in.

You might use some of the communication skills described in chapter 4. What communication tips do you each want to remember when you take this time to repair what happened and better understand each other? Write down in your notebook what comes to mind.

Examples of Time-Out Agreements

Here's an example of a time-out agreement made by Thomas and Marina.

How We Ask for a Time-Out:

When one of us feels too overwhelmed or triggered to continue the conversation, we will do our best to say "I love you and I need a pause to love you better."

What We Want Each Other to Know and Remember During the Time-Out:

Marina—I want Thomas to know that I am more sensitive to triggers since becoming a mom and this isn't his fault. It's important to me to show up in a loving way and taking space helps me do this. I know the space is hard for him and I promise I will come back and not avoid or emotionally abandon him.

Thomas—I want Marina to know that it's okay to take the space she needs even though in the past it's been hard for me to be patient when she needs space. I know that taking the space helps her feel safe and that is important to me. I will work on being patient so that I can be a better partner.

How Long Our Time-Out Will Last:

Because of our work schedules and parenting responsibilities, the best time for us to connect is when the baby goes down to sleep at night. We will plan to return to the discussion at this time. We will do our best to be kind and respectful in our interactions with each other throughout the time in between our triggering moment and our discussion because we depend on each other throughout the day—but we will not initiate the triggering topic before our decided time.

How We Will Soothe Ourselves:

Marina—I will take a walk outside with the baby, journal, or call my best friend. I will not use the phone call to vent or complain about Thomas if I do call my friend.

Thomas—I will practice the mindful self-compassion skills I've been using and use my mindfulness app, which helps me relax my body through breathing and meditation.

When We Come Back Together:

Marina—I will practice not dismissing Thomas's feelings. I will do my best to use the validation and empathy communication tips I've been working on.

Thomas—I will work hard to use "I-statements" instead of blaming or criticizing Marina because I know it just pushes her away more when I communicate like I used to.

And here's another example of a time-out agreement, this time between Gia and Samantha.

How We Ask for a Time-Out:

We will use the American Sign Language sign for "I love you" and ask for a time-out.

What We Want Each Other to Know and Remember During the Time-Out:

Gia—I want Samantha to know that even though I can get triggered by her anger, I know that her anger is coming from a place that wants to protect me and our relationship. I want her to know that taking a pause helps me ground myself so I can come back and support her with her anger instead of becoming scared of it.

Samantha—I want Gia to know that I know my anger scares her and makes it hard for her to open up to me. I am working to ask for a pause before the anger becomes too overwhelming so that I feel more grounded when I talk to her. Keeping her emotionally safe is important to me.

How Long Our Time-Out Will Last:
We will schedule our "come back together time" when we ask for a timeout. We will do our best to never walk away from a triggering interaction without scheduling this time. If we do forget to schedule it though, either of us can check in with the other about whether it's a good time once forty-five minutes or more have passed.

How We Will Soothe Ourselves:
Gia—I will use the soothing exercises I learned in therapy or take our dog to the park.

Samantha—I will journal about my anger, which usually ends in a good cry. If I can't sit down to journal, I'll go for a run.

When We Come Back Together:
Gia—I will use the breathing skills I've learned to keep my body calm during our talk so I don't shut down or dissociate. I will focus on creating positive connection between us, but I will be honest

if I start dissociating so that Samantha doesn't feel abandoned.

Samantha—I will work on opening up about the more vulnerable feelings that cause my anger.

As you see from the examples, a time-out agreement gives partners struggling with the effects of sexual trauma a structure in which to make sure each partner's needs and the needs of the relationship are met even when things might be hard. That said, there will definitely be moments when you or your partner is not able to hit the pause button before you do or say something that triggers the other partner. No matter how much work you do to soothe yourselves, you will lose control or misstep because you are human and imperfect.

Repairing Relationship Ruptures After Triggering Moments

A relationship feels secure not because we always get things right; it's secure because when we know we've done something to hurt our partner, we are able to come back together and repair the hurt together. When relationship ruptures happen—one of you loses your temper, yells, is passive-aggressive, behaves hurtfully, or just shuts down in a way that leaves the other feeling unsupported—here are some tips you can use for the work of relationship repair.

Use communication skills discussed in chapter 4. The communication skills in chapter 4 are useful any time we are communicating! They are particularly helpful when we want to create a sense of connection and safety for the person we are talking to. *What skills in chapter 4 are you already using? What skills do you want to make a conscious effort to practice more often?*

Be curious about your partner's experience. We all want our partners to understand us! And we can also jump right in to telling our partner what we think about our interaction without taking the time to explore what was going on for them when they were triggered or there was a relationship rupture. If you're working to repair a rupture with your partner, you might ask them how they felt, what was going on for them, what triggered them, or how they felt when you said or did certain things. If they are not making sense to you, stay curious as you listen and put yourself in their shoes. Even if you wouldn't feel the way they felt, their responses make sense based on their own experiences and sensitive parts.

Validate their feelings and show them you understand your impact on them. Let your partner know what does make sense to you. Own your role in the rupture. It's so important to let our loved ones know that even if we didn't mean to hurt them, we see that we did and we want to comfort them when this happens.

Open up about your experience and ask for any reassurance you need. Share what was going on for you in your rupture—your feelings, fears—and what comfort or reassurance you need from your partner now to help you move on from the rupture.

Reassure your partner that you care about them and you're glad they can open up to you about what triggered them. Thank your partner for taking the time to have this discussion with you. Repairing ruptures is hard work, and showing gratitude helps us return to this practice again and again in the future.

Brainstorm what you can do differently next time. Now that you have a better understanding of your impact on your partner, brainstorm together about what you two can do next time you get triggered in a similar way.

Come to an agreement on the story of the rupture, if possible. When we have a shared understanding of a difficult experience, we feel more connected and like we are on the same team. The worksheet below will help you do this.

Remind each other that triggers happen and it's okay. We can feel guilty and even ashamed when we fall back into cycles of disconnection. The reality is, no relationship avoids triggers all the time. Reassuring each other that this is normal can be helpful.

At http://www.newharbinger.com/51574, you'll find a "Rupture Repair Worksheet" that will help you put these tips into practice by allowing you to explore, in moments of conflict, (1) what happened, (2) the actions you Worksheet" that will help you put these tips into practice by allowing you to explore, in moments of conflict, (1) what happened, (2) the actions you took, (3) the actions your partner took, (4) your feelings, (5) your partner's feelings, (6) your fears, (7) your partner's fears, (8) the reassurance you needed in that moment and in similar ones in the future, (9) the reassurance your partner needed, and finally, (10) what you'd like to do differently next time.

Here's what Thomas and Marina's relationship repair process looked like, as they worked through each step.

What happened?

Briefly describe what happened from start to finish.

We went out to dinner for our anniversary and got a babysitter. We had a nice night and it was implied that we would have sex when we got home. When we got home the babysitter was pacing the house with our crying baby. Thomas rolled his eyes and went to bed while Marina cared for the baby for a couple of hours before she went to sleep. When Marina came to bed, Thomas was already sleeping and hadn't said goodnight to Marina. We didn't discuss what happened that night, but we both felt the tension and had unsaid feelings.

Our Actions

Take ownership for your own role in the cycle. What did each of you do and why?

Thomas's actions: I was passive-aggressive with the eyeroll and I shut down. Even though I could say that I went to bed without saying goodnight because Marina was busy with the baby, I know that part of me was wanting to ignore her so she could feel how I feel in these moments.

Marina's actions: I swooped right in to take care of our daughter without saying anything to Thomas or acknowledging that our plans would need to be postponed. I didn't offer Thomas any gratitude for the night or reassurance that I look forward to a raincheck.

Our Feelings

Reflect on all the different feelings you each had in the conflict.

Thomas's feelings: I felt sad, alone, surprised, and frustrated.

Marina's feelings: I felt overwhelmed by the baby, frustrated, and guilty.

Our Fears

Reflect on everything you were worried about during the interaction.

Thomas's fears: I was worried Marina was grateful that sex with me got postponed. I know that the baby needed her, but what if she felt relief that our night ended early?

Marina's fears: I was worried that Thomas was mad at me and that I'll never get it right with him. I was also a little frustrated I was left alone to care for the baby when we realized she was still up. I really enjoyed our anniversary dinner and was looking forward to having some alone time in the bedroom.

Our Needs for Reassurance

How would you each like your partner to reassure you when you feel this way?

Reassurance Thomas needs: That I matter to her and am special to her. That it's not a chore to connect with me.

Reassurance Marina needs: That he sees all the ways I reach for him and try to connect. That he's willing to meet me halfway and help me when I need it so we can both get what we want. That we'll still be okay when we have ruptures like this.

What We'd Like to Do Differently Next Time

This is the shared agreement on how you will try to do things next time.

Thomas will work on being more gentle when plans get thrown off and when asking Marina for reassurance before he shuts down; he also will try to be a more supportive coparent. Marina will practice acknowledging Thomas, even if it's just a quick smile and kiss, when her attention gets pulled quickly away from the relationship.

Putting It All Together

Setting an expectation that you will never hurt your partner or trigger them isn't helpful because this happens in all relationships. If you have turned to this book, this has likely been happening all too frequently, leaving you feeling very overwhelmed! The more you practice understanding each other's triggers without becoming too defensive, taking time-outs when needed, and repairing these ruptures when necessary, the less likely you will experience these painful moments. And when they do happen—because they will—you will feel less activated and more confident as you navigate the road map back to a relaxed and connected state of being. And speaking of connected, in the next chapter we will talk about how to have a healthy sexual connection with your partner.

CHAPTER 6

Establishing (or Regaining) Intimate Connection and Pleasure

All relationships have sexual ups and downs. It's normal for you to experience times in your relationship when sex flows easily, times when one or both of you notice it isn't happening as naturally, and times when changes to your bodies or experiences make sex more uncomfortable—or at least require more effort.

Not all sexual trauma survivors report that they experience distress or concerns in their sex life. A survivor of a sexually abusive relationship, for instance, may report that they feel free and safe with their next partner who is not abusive. A survivor of childhood molestation may notice that they dissociate at times during sex—and they may or may not have a problem with this. A survivor of rape may share that sex is hard for them in new relationships, but once trust is built it becomes easier. Which is to say: survivor experiences vary and can change over time. And it's important that we take our partner's lead and trust what they tell us they are or aren't experiencing before we make any assumptions.

At the time of reading this book, you may be experiencing a satisfying sex life, experiencing normal ups and downs of a long-term relationship, or one or both of you may have anxiety around sex due to sexual trauma or other negative sexual experiences in the past. Because the survivor experience can vary, the tips and exercises in this chapter are written to benefit any sexual relationship—but they do need to be used with care. This involves an awareness of what trauma responses can look like and a willingness to stop, check in, and prioritize the experience your partner's having at any given moment, especially if they're triggered.

There are so many important issues to discuss surrounding sexual intimacy—including creating safety, dealing with stress and conflict, and establishing and respecting boundaries—which we'll address in this chapter. I'll also help you articulate your vision for a healthy sex life, discuss advantages of scheduling sex, provide bonding questions to enhance your sexual relationship, and offer exercises to promote intimacy and pleasure. If either you or your partner gets triggered to a trauma response during any activities or discussions in this chapter, be sure to stop the activity immediately and use skills you've learned in chapters 3, 4, and 5. You might decide together to use stress reduction tips from chapter 3, relationship skills from chapter 4, or skills for coping with triggers from chapter 5. You can use any of these skills before, during, or after physical intimacy to help diminish the likelihood of being triggered to a trauma response.

Tips for Reading This Chapter

You might read this chapter alone or share it with your partner. I hope the information and exercises will help you build even more safety and trust in your relationship, and that through conversations and activities you experience more pleasure and joy in your sex life.

Sometimes our partners don't want to work on improving their sex life; sometimes we ourselves don't want to. If your partner has shared that they are not interested in improving your sex life, you might feel rejected and hurt, especially if sexual connection helps you feel secure and loved in your relationship. It's okay to let your partner know that improving sexual connection is important to you, and you have to also respect their boundaries here without pressuring them to change. Consent is important even in conversations. Topics and activities that seem harmless and non-triggering to you may be very overwhelming to your partner.

If you think it might be helpful for your partner to read this chapter, you might ask them whether they are willing to read it and whether they are open to doing any of the suggested activities. If they are not fully on board, though, respect their boundary and ask them to let you know whether or when this changes for them.

If you two do decide to dive into some of these activities, remember that slower is better when your survivor partner is re-establishing connection to their own body and yours. If you move too quickly, push through feelings of overwhelm or anxiety, or ignore times that your partner needs to slow down or stop, you risk hurting or retraumatizing them. Reassure your partner that they can slow down, pause, or stop at any time. Check in with them throughout the activities and especially if you see any signs of distress. And when your partner opens up about their feelings, use the empathy and validation skills you learned in chapter 4 to support them.

Creating Safety

Have you ever had someone tease or criticize you during or after sexual intimacy? What about touching or entering you without warning in a way that catches you off guard? Whether you've experienced sexual trauma or not, if you've ever had experiences that caused you to feel anxious, confused, overwhelmed, or hurt, you'll know the kinds of feelings that can contribute to less safety in a sexual relationship. Creating a sense of safety isn't only an important aspect of physical intimacy for sexual trauma survivors. We all benefit when we feel safe during sex.

That said, it's particularly important to help your partner feel safe during physical intimacy because their safety was taken from them during their sexual trauma. You may already be doing things that create safety for your partner without even knowing it! Or it might seem like sometimes your partner feels safe and relaxed during sex and sometimes they don't.

One thing that can be helpful no matter where you and your partner are in your relationship is to check in with them to get a baseline about how safe they feel during intimacy and whether there's anything you could do differently to support them.

EXERCISE: Having a Conversation About Safety

Ask your partner whether they are open to having a conversation about physical intimacy so you can learn more about their sexual needs. If they are open to having the conversation, let them know that it's okay if they want to pause or stop the conversation at any time. Let them know that it's okay if they don't have the answers to the questions you want to ask and it's also okay if they want to think about it and come back to you. Finally, let them know that you are learning that everyone has different needs to help them feel safe and relaxed during physical intimacy and you are curious about what needs your partner has.

You might ask them one or all of the following questions:

What helps you feel safe with me?

Is there anything I'm already doing before, during, or after physical intimacy that helps you feel safe?

Is there anything I'm doing in those moments that causes you to feel less safe?

Is there anything you'd like me to start doing or do more of to help you feel safe?

Your partner's answers may change over time. You can return to these questions any time you sense they are more anxious or triggered during intimacy to help you better understand and support them.

Dealing with Stress and Conflict

Two issues that significantly affect sexual connection and intimacy are stress and conflict within the relationship. We touched on stress reduction earlier in the book as an important part of self-care and emotional connection. High stress in our lives can also lead to us wanting sex less. We might avoid it altogether, experience less pleasure, or rely on sex strictly as a destressing activity instead of a way to connect with someone we love.

EXERCISE: Stress Check-Up

You can do this activity alone or together with your partner. There are two goals of this activity: become aware of how much stress you're holding and make plans to decrease the stress.

1. On a scale of 1–10, with 1 being the least amount of stress you can experience and 10 being the most, how are you currently ranking on the following areas of your life?
   - Work stress
   - Parenting stress
   - Extended family stress
   - Social stress (activities, social commitments)
   - Health stress
   - Relationship stress
   - Financial stress
   - Stress from oppression or global/political issues
   - Spiritual stress
2. Consider whether you tend to avoid sex when you are stressed or want it more as a stress relief. How is this impacting you and your relationship?
3. Identify any changes you want to make to reduce stress in any of the above areas of your life. This might include saying no to invitations, setting boundaries in different

areas of your life, or using any of the stress reduction techniques outlined in chapter 3.

In addition to stress, it's normal and healthy for there to be conflict in our relationships. Conflict can even bring us closer together when we take time to understand our different perspectives and work together to find resolution or acceptance of our differences. But if there are certain issues that create overwhelming conflict in the relationship and lead to disrespectful communication or drive us to avoid opening up about our concerns, it often becomes harder to feel comfortable getting close enough to our partners to improve our sex lives.

If you are noticing that you and your partner are having too much relationship conflict, return to the activities in chapter 4 and use the communication techniques to move toward more understanding of each other. If you continue to get stuck, you may consider reaching out for couples therapy.

Although it is possible to have a sexual relationship while you are having conflict with your partner, it could contribute to stress, avoidance of each other, and less feelings of security in the relationship that makes sex less enjoyable or off the table altogether.

Establishing Sexual Boundaries

We all have different boundaries around touch and sex, and it's normal for our boundaries to change over time. Say we have an injury and we can no longer enjoy a favorite sexual position. Or we give birth and need more foreplay before penetration once our bodies heal. Or we used to be a hard no for oral sex, but something changes and that boundary loosens. Partners with healthy sex lives can communicate their boundaries to each other and continue to communicate those boundaries as they change.

Your partner might have boundaries that are directly related to their sexual trauma, or they might be boundaries that they'd have without the trauma ever having taken place. Try not to think of their boundaries as "temporary until they heal their trauma" because that mindset may lead you to disappointment and frustration. What's more, when you accept and respect your partner's boundaries without questioning, negotiating, or hoping for them to change, you can create safety and connection in your relationship.

With that in mind, see whether you can invite your partner to share more with you about their boundaries.

EXERCISE: Reflecting on Boundaries, Together

Before you embark on the steps that follow, take a second to think about your own boundaries around sex and intimacy. When it comes to physical touch and sexual intimacy, what do you like? And what would you rather not do? Thinking about these questions at the outset can set the stage for the conversation to follow.

Then, ask your partner whether they are open to having a conversation about sexual boundaries so you can learn more about their sexual needs. Just as in the conversation about safety, if they are open to having a conversation about boundaries, let them know that it's okay if they want to pause or stop the conversation at any time. Let them know that it's okay if they don't have the answers to the questions you want to ask and it's also okay if they want to think about it and come back to you. Finally, let them know that you are learning that everyone has different sexual boundaries and they may change over time. You want to learn more about theirs so you can respect their needs.

You might ask them one or all of the following questions:

> What physical touch and sexual boundaries do you have? (Examples: no vaginal penetration without a condom, not being touched from behind when I can't see you, not touching me sexually when there are people around, not initiating anal penetration without verbal consent each time)

> Do you feel comfortable letting me know your boundaries as they come up? If not, what

can I do to help you feel comfortable coming to me and letting me know?

Do you feel comfortable in knowing what my boundaries are? Would you like me to tell you some of them?

Is there anything else you'd like to tell me on this topic?

You can return to these questions any time you sense that your partner is more anxious or triggered during intimacy to help you better understand and support them.

Creating a Vision for a Healthy Sex Life

How much sex do you and your partner want to be having? What do you want your sex life to look like? There isn't a normal number of times to have sex a month. In fact, while most folks report a decrease in relationship satisfaction when they are having sex fewer than two times a month, there is no significant increase in relationship satisfaction for couples having sex more than two to four times a month.

It's also true that our libidos can wax and wane over time. All in all, it's helpful for the two of you to check in with each other on a regular basis about what feels good in the relationship. This activity will help you start that conversation.

EXERCISE: Creating Your Vision for a Healthy Sex Life

For this activity, each of you will reflect on the following questions and then share your answers. Use your conversation skills from chapter 4 as together you envision what a healthy sex life looks like in your current relationship.

With our current values and relationship priorities in mind, how many times would you like us to have intercourse a month?

What experiences of sexual and physical connection, including but not limited to sex, are most important to you to prioritize? (Examples: romance in our relationship, cuddles and kisses most nights even without intercourse, more playfulness or trying new things)

If we have differences in our visions, how can we compromise?

How can we plan to put our shared vision into action?

Scheduling Sex and Intimacy

I often suggest to couples I work with that they start scheduling times for intimacy and sex. And I almost always get pushback initially:

"Scheduling will take out the spontaneity that makes sex fun!"

"Scheduling makes it seem like a chore—I want sex to happen because we both want it to, not because it's another thing on the calendar."

"If we have to schedule sex, it's a sign that we're not sexually compatible."

I disagree with all of these statements.

If sex is a priority in a relationship, we need to commit to it, as we would with any relationship priority, and protect our time so it doesn't keep getting pushed to the bottom of our to-do list.

We also are more likely to have sex when it's scheduled because both people can mentally prepare for it. If we wait for sex to happen spontaneously, we're much more likely to catch our partner off guard when we pursue them—then we can get in a cycle of feeling rejected and not pursuing as much. Scheduling sex lets us take the pressure off of this dynamic and can create safety and trust for both partners.

All we're doing when we schedule sex is planning for our time together. You were likely doing this when your relationship first became sexual, too, though you likely weren't thinking about it as scheduling sex. When we first start having sex in a relationship, we think about how we'll likely have sex when we see each other or the next time we are in bed together. We don't pull out our phones and schedule sex on the calendar, but there is a sometimes-unspoken agreement that our time together will lead to sex, which allows us to mentally prepare. And mentally preparing (fantasizing, looking forward to it, wearing clothes we feel sexy in, flirting with each other) all help the sexual connection feel more enjoyable.

With these points in mind, consider scheduling in sex and intimacy with each other and notice how it affects you.

Bonding Questions for Better Sex

Even though it can seem like sex is everywhere—in movies and TV shows, song lyrics, the news—our society still doesn't do a very good job of helping us feel normal talking about sex in our relationships. So much is happening inside of our heads and bodies, in intimate moments, that we don't discuss with our sexual partners. If we do take steps to open up about what's going on inside before, during, and after sex, our partner can both get to know us on a deeper level and do a better job of meeting our sexual needs.

This section of the book includes questions and prompts so you and your partner can get to know each other better. I've used questions just like these with couples who have been together for decades, and they still were surprised by how much they learned about each other and how much more comfortable and enjoyable intimacy became after these conversations. It's never too late to bond sexually in this way!

Before diving into these questions, make sure you are both 100% on board with the activity. I don't suggest working through all the questions in one session, but maybe spending twenty to forty minutes each time you sit down to talk. Make a plan together of when you will discuss these questions, where you will do so (hopefully a private space away from distraction and interruption), and how either of you can veto a question or pause if needed.

There are three sections: turn-ons and turnoffs, fantasies and memories, and preferences for how you'd like to pursue or be pursued. Each section involves a phase of self-reflection and a phase in which you open up to your partner if you feel comfortable doing so. If you do not feel comfortable opening up or even self-reflecting on a certain topic yet, skip that section. If you wish you felt more comfortable opening up, still skip the section for now but reflect on what you might need in order to feel safer. Share that with your partner if you wish, and try to work together to create that safety.

Turn-Ons and Turnoffs

Let's look at the various ways we are turned on or turned off. We might be impacted by our environment, our bodies, our senses, and our experiences and desires.

Our Environment
- Do you like the lights turned on or off? Or does it vary?
- What locations have we had sex in that turn you on? Examples include:
  - Bedroom feels sexy to me!
  - Against a wall is a turn-on.
  - Shower
  - The car
  - When we're staying over someplace new or at someone's house
  - Other:
- Are there any locations that turn you off?
- Are there any locations you want to experiment with?

Your Body
- What parts of your body feel most sexual to you?
  - Face (be specific: eyes, lips, cheeks, nose?)
  - Hair
  - Neck, throat
  - Shoulders, arms
  - Hands
  - Chest
  - Back
  - Waist
  - Butt
  - Genitals
  - Upper legs
  - Calves

- Feet
- What parts of my body feel most sexual to you or turn you on?
  - Face (be specific: eyes, lips, cheeks, nose?)
    - Hair
    - Neck, throat
    - Shoulders, arms
    - Hands
    - Chest
    - Back
    - Waist
    - Butt
    - Genitals
    - Upper legs
    - Calves
    - Feet
- What feels more sexy, being fully naked or partially clothed?
- What parts of your body feel unsexy?

Touch
- Where do you like to be touched?
  - Face (be specific: eyes, lips, cheeks, nose?)
    - Hair
    - Neck, throat
    - Shoulders, arms
    - Hands
    - Chest
    - Back
    - Waist

- Butt
- Genitals
- Upper legs
- Calves
- Feet
- How do you like to be touched?
  - Soft
  - Firm
  - Medium
  - Massage
  - Grab
  - Spank
  - Hold
  - Hug
  - Tickle
  - Other:
- What do you like to touch/feel during sex?
  - Your own body (be specific)
  - Your partner's body (be specific)
  - Toys
  - Pillows
  - Other:
- Are there any turn-offs in how I touch you?
  - Soft
  - Firm
  - Medium
  - Massage
  - Grab
  - Spank
  - Hold
  - Hug

- Tickle
- Other:
- Is there anything you don't like to touch?
- Is there anything you would like to add to the touch/feel experience of having sex?

Scent
- Are there any smells during sex that turn you on?
  - The scent of my natural skin
  - The scent of my cologne/perfume/body wash/hair wash
  - The scent of my genitals or sexual fluids
  - A lotion, oil, or lubrication you like
  - A certain candle smell or room scent
  - Fresh sheets on the bed
  - Other:
- Are there any smells during sex that turn you off?
  - Bad breath
  - Body odor if unshowered
  - Other:
- Is there anything you would like to add to the scent experience of sex?
  - Start lighting a candle
  - Add a scented massage oil for foreplay
  - Make sure we both brush our teeth
  - Other:

Sight

- Do you like having your eyes open or closed during sex? Does it vary?
- If you like having your eyes closed, is there anything you would like me to do or not do when your eyes are closed?
- What do you like to look at during sex?
- Is there anything you would like to add to the visual experience of sex?

Sound
- What sounds of sex turn you on?
    - Our bodies
    - Dirty talk
    - Sounds I make that show I'm experiencing pleasure
    - Music playing
    - Other:
- What sounds turn you off?
    - Hearing the pets, children in another room
    - Complete silence
    - Anything from the above list
    - Other:
- Do you like dirty talk? If so, what kind?
- Are there any sounds you'd like to add to our sexual experiences?
- Are there any sounds that are distracting during sex that you'd like to find ways to limit?

Taste

- What tastes do you like to experience during sex?
    - My mouth
    - My skin
    - My genitals
    - My sexual fluid
    - Food play: chocolate, whipped cream, fruit
    - Flavored lubricant, edible oils
    - Other:
- What tastes turn you off?
- Is there anything you would like to add to the taste experience of sex with each other?

Control

- Do you get turned on by taking control during sex (with consent)?
- Do you get turned on when your partner takes control during sex (with consent)?
- What ways can you or I take control during sex that would turn you on?

Relaxation

- What helps you relax before sex so you can be present and open for the experience?
    - Knowing when we're going to have it so you can prepare
    - A shower
    - Reading or watching something sensual
    - Dancing together
    - Going on a date

- Having a bonding or emotionally connecting conversation
  - Other:
- How can I help you relax before sex?

Foreplay
- What do you like for foreplay?
  - Sexy texts—no pictures, please
  - Sexy texts—pictures welcome
  - Flirting before or throughout the day
  - Make-out session
  - Dry humping
  - Teasing penetration
  - Massage
  - Side-by-side masturbation
  - Use of toys, kink play
  - Tickles
  - Dancing
  - Striptease
  - Role-play
  - Having a bonding or emotionally connecting conversation
  - Other:
- How much foreplay do you like or need to help you become aroused or ready for intercourse?

Aftercare
- What do you like after sex?
  - Cuddling
  - To be able to clean my body discreetly
  - A shower

- Checking in
- Meditation
- Sleep
- Spooning
- Eating something
- Other:

- How can you feel cared for and appreciated by me after we are intimate?
- Is there anything I do after sex or intimacy that makes you uncomfortable or feels like a rejection?

Fantasies and Memories

The questions in this section are aimed at learning about each other's sexual fantasies and memories.

- Do you have sex dreams? Are there any you'd like to share with me?
- Do you have a favorite fantasy? Would you like to share it with me? Would you like to try to create elements of it?
- What is your favorite sexual experience with me?
- Do you masturbate, and if so, what helps you become aroused or orgasm through masturbation?
- Is there anything else you need from me to help you achieve orgasm during intimacy?

Pursuing Each Other

Finally, this section poses questions to help you and your partner learn about your preferences related to pursuing one another for physical intimacy.

- When you are thinking about initiating physical intimacy, is there anything you are nervous about?
- Is there any reassurance you need to help you feel more comfortable initiating physical intimacy?
- If I am going to initiate physical intimacy with you, do you have any tips on ways you would like me to initiate?
- If I initiate physical intimacy and you are not in the mood (whatever the reason), how do you feel? Is there anything you want me to know about how you feel in those moments?
- If I am not interested or able to be physically intimate with you, how would you like me to decline? Is there any reassurance you might need?
- What if I am open to physical intimacy after you initiate, but I'm not sure how far I want to go or whether I want to have intercourse? How can I communicate this with you?

You will each learn so much about each other as you explore these questions together.

It may feel quite awkward or uncomfortable at first, but it will get easier with time.

Exercises That Promote Intimacy and Increase Pleasure

This section of the chapter introduces exercises that will help you increase the bonding hormones that are naturally produced during times of physical intimacy. You'll also notice an emphasis in these activities on the qualities of presence and mindfulness—nonjudgmental attention to whatever's arising for you in a given moment—that you've practiced throughout this book. When you practice being present in your body and with your partner, you create a sense of security while also increasing your own experience of pleasure and love.

Just as you did in the last section, before diving into these activities, make sure you are both 100% on board. Do not try to cram all of these activities into one day, or even one week or one month. I recommend spending twenty to forty-five minutes two or three times a week and being flexible if that becomes too much or some exercises are too overwhelming to start right away. Plan together when you will practice these exercises, where you will do so (hopefully a private space away from distraction and interruption), and how either of you can veto an exercise or pause if needed.

Also, keep in mind that these exercises will be most effective when your relationship has a secure foundation. If you're currently stuck in a cycle of triggering either of your attachment reactions and disconnection cycle, it's best to return to the emotional work of building that secure attachment in your relationship before you introduce physical bonding exercises. If you have done your best to use the skills you're learning in this book but still notice your disconnection cycle is feeling unmanageable, you might consider getting help from a relationship therapist.

You'll also need a good amount of physical safety for both partners to introduce these exercises. Physical safety might look like trusting that your partner will support you if you need to pause or stop intimacy when you are overwhelmed without pressuring, coercing, or emotionally attacking each other. If either partner does not feel physically safe in the relationship, these activities can feel overwhelming and triggering.

Finally, if you feel physically and emotionally secure in your relationship but these activities are still anxiety provoking—that is okay and normal! You might feel silly, awkward, shy, excited, nervous, or even worried that your partner won't enjoy being with you in these exercises. As long as you are willing to try the activities and you're not scared of being hurt, I encourage you to notice these feelings and accept them as normal while you turn your attention back to the exercise and being with your partner.

EXERCISE: Eye Gazing

Gazing into a loving person's eyes can soothe us and give us a rush of bonding hormones. Think about how a parent gazes into their newborn's eyes when they feed or cuddle them; it is through our gaze that we first learn to communicate and be close with others. Studies also show that a loving gaze is something that we almost only experience in romantic partnerships, caregiving relationships (e.g., parent-child, grandparent-grandchild), and with our pets. It's a marker of attachment and helps regulate our nervous system.

At first, try this exercise once a day for a week. For the first two times, you might try two minutes. Then move to trying to stay with each other's gaze for five minutes and notice how you feel. After you practice this mindfully for a week, decide together how you would like to integrate this into your connection practices. Do you want to return to it as needed, practice it once a week, use it as part of your foreplay? It is up to you.

- Choose a private and comfortable place in your home to practice this exercise. It should be away from distractions and interruptions.

- Put your phones on silent if they are in the room.
- Make sure you can comfortably face each other without back pain or leg cramping so that you can be present with each other without frequent repositioning.
- Use a timer or an alarm on a phone or watch so that you do not have to check a clock during the exercise. Make sure the buzz or chime isn't too loud or annoying so that you don't get triggered from the sound when it goes off.
- Breathe deeply, relax your body, and notice how it feels to gaze at each other.
- It might feel silly, awkward, or funny—that's okay! Relax into it and know that anything you feel is normal.
- If you notice yourself getting distracted by your thoughts, just notice that and return your attention back to your partner's eyes and loving gaze.
- Notice any sensations you feel in your body; try to sit with love and an open heart.

EXERCISE: *Love Your Body*

Loving our bodies isn't always easy or possible. Sometimes, we struggle so much with body image that it creates anxiety during sex. We might avoid looking at our own bodies, feel anxious when our bodies are touched, or try not to be seen naked or partially clothed.

In this exercise, you'll work to move toward body acceptance and appreciation as much as possible. It also helps you get used to thinking about or being present with your body. You don't need to feel unconditional love and appreciation for your body at all times, but activities like these help move you toward a more secure connection with your body overall and help you feel more comfortable being physically close and vulnerable with your partner.

Part of the exercise will involve you focusing on your own body, and part of the exercise will focus on giving appreciation to your partner's body.

Part 1: Self

While looking at yourself in the mirror (clothed or naked), think about what you appreciate about your body. Take deep breaths and stay positive in your thinking even if you feel nervous or uncomfortable. Try to do this once a week.

Examples of body appreciation statements:
- I love my arms because they hold my child.
- I love my legs because they take me on walks.
- I love my eyes because they help me see beautiful things in the world.

Part 2: Together

At a time when you can both relax and focus on each other, share appreciation and love for your partner's body.

Examples of body appreciation statements:
- I love your arms because they feel strong when they hold me.
- I love your breasts because they feel tender in my hands.
- I love your eyes because when I gaze into them my heart fills with love.

It might be hard to hear the compliments from your partner; you might find resistance or disagreement coming up instinctively. Breathe deeply and try to accept the words.

EXERCISE: *Noticing Pleasure*

This activity uses mindfulness to help you notice pleasure. We have experiences all day every day that would feel pleasurable to us if we slowed down and practiced being in the moment. The more we slow down, connect to our senses, and feel the pleasure in the moment, the more sensitive we become to noticing pleasure throughout the day. This creates a positive cycle of inviting pleasure in, feeling more heightened pleasure, and seeking more pleasurable moments throughout our day (including pleasure of a sexual nature).

Try to do the following every day. The more you connect with pleasure on a regular basis, the more your body opens up to pleasure and relaxation. Use this skill alone and in moments with your partner.

- Practice mindful connection to your own body and pleasurable sensations at different times of the day.
- Engage your senses: the pleasure of tasting your coffee in the morning, the pleasure of feeling the water hit your body in the shower, the pleasure of the scent of clean laundry, the pleasure of looking at a beautiful piece of art, the pleasure of listening to your favorite song.

EXERCISE: Sensual Touch and Mindfulness

This activity is based on sensate focus exercises developed by researchers William Masters and Virginia Johnson in the 1960s, which were the first research-based interventions to support couples experiencing sexual problems (Masters, Johnson, and Kolodny 1994). The goal of this activity is to increase pleasure experienced during touch, decrease anxiety either partner feels during sexual intimacy, and connect or reconnect partners sexually in a secure way.

The exercise involves taking turns sensually caressing, stroking, and feeling your partner's body. Try this two or three times a week for twenty minutes.

Before you start:
- Discuss where and when you will do these exercises and what will help both of you focus and feel relaxed. Consider a place and time you won't be interrupted, a time of day that works for both of you, how you can consistently practice two or three times a week, and whether you would like to add anything for comfort (lights on/off, music on/off, candle burning).
- Agree on whether you would like to start fully clothed, lightly clothed, or naked (you can decide together when to progress).
- Note that sexual intercourse is off the table during the twenty-minute exercise, and it's not an expectation afterward. Discuss whether you would like intercourse to be completely off the table or whether it would be okay if it leads to intercourse afterward.

Now, here are guidelines for the exercise:
- For the first week, start with focusing only on hands, arms, feet, and legs; from there, you can progress to adding different body parts, including erotic zones and genitals. Discuss together before each exercise what

you would like to add or whether you would like to stay at the same stage.
- Split the twenty-minute time into two ten-minute periods. One of you will be the receiver of touch and one will be the giver of touch for each period. Take turns going first as the giver of touch (you can switch every time or each week).
- Focus is an important part of the activity because you will work to focus on your *own* sensations instead of what you think your partner is thinking or feeling, whether you are the giver or the receiver of touch. Do what feels good to you and focus on your own feelings; do not focus on trying to please your partner when you are the giver of touch.
- Share with each other any areas you do not want to be touched if it will be intolerable (like if you are very ticklish somewhere).
- Do not give feedback during the activity; just notice your own sensations.
- If you notice your mind going to thoughts such as *Am I doing this right? Do they like this?* or *I don't like how they are doing this*, try to just notice those thoughts and then return your attention to the sensations.
- Afterward, only share positive feedback or something you noticed about the exercise.

Do not share what you didn't like or what you wish your partner did differently immediately after the activity because the focus of the activity is meant to move you away from critiques or performance anxiety. Instead, share things like "I liked how it felt when you touched my fingertips" or "I noticed it felt like time was moving slowly in the beginning, but then I felt really relaxed."

Putting It All together

Sexual intimacy is a chance to bond with each other on a deep level, and it can feel like sexual trauma is a barrier to a spontaneous and enjoyable connection. It doesn't need to be this way. The safer we feel in our relationships and the clearer we are about our boundaries and sexual expectations, the more likely we will be able to connect intimately. Give yourselves permission for imperfect sex, for good enough sex, for sex without penetration, for sex that turns into cuddling, for sex that feels silly, for a slow sexual connection that builds safety and love while helping to heal the sexual trauma that came before.

CHAPTER 7

Stages of Healing and Hope for the Future

You have learned so much in this book, and hopefully you and your partner are beginning to see the benefit if you have put some of these tips and approaches into use. Before we say goodbye, we will review the common stages that a sexual trauma survivor goes through in their healing and how you can support them. We'll also discuss how you can help end sexual trauma by practicing allyship and confronting rape culture. Finally, we will hear from survivors and their partners as they share windows into their experiences and provide hope for the future of your and your partner's healing.

Stages of Survivor Healing

Just as each person is unique, the road to healing for survivors will look different for everyone. There are common stages after sexual trauma that you or your partner may recognize. Remember that their path might not be linear; they may visit different stages of healing during different times or stay in certain stages for days or years. They might even not visit certain stages at all, and that's okay! Read about each stage below and how you can support your and your partner's healing from their trauma when they are in each stage.

Shock/Denial/Disorientation

After being sexual assaulted, many survivors experience a stage of shock, denial, and/or disorientation. In chapter 1, you learned about shock, numbness, and avoidance as being a common emotional experience of survivors of sexual assault. You can support your partner through this first phase of healing by respecting any boundaries or needs they communicate. You can offer to check in on them or stay accessible to them so they feel less alone. If your partner is in this stage of healing, they may or may not be interested in making a police report or seeking medical attention. You can offer to help them do these things, but it's important to respect their requests.

Initial Adjustment

During this stage of healing, a survivor and their support system may have taken initial steps to help manage the impact of the trauma. If your partner is in this stage, they may or may not appear to be doing better and distancing themselves from people, places, and activities that increase their distress. You can support your partner in this stage by refraining from putting pressure on them to return to life as normal. Let them know that it's okay and normal to have ups and downs during this time and that they don't need to keep their negative thoughts or emotions to themself if they don't want to.

Reexperiencing and Increase in Trauma Symptoms

Most of this book is written with a survivor going through this phase of healing in mind. As you've learned, there are many different symptoms a survivor of trauma may experience, and many ways to support them in their healing, depending on what they are experiencing. In other words, there is no specific guidance I can give you for this stage of healing; rather, apply the tips and strategies you have learned and practiced throughout this book to support your partner in this phase depending on their needs. Remember, having discussions and obtaining consent apply for any strategy you think might be helpful.

Seeking Support

Survivors may or may not reach out for support when they feel stuck in their healing. Your partner may turn to only you for support, or they might turn to friends, support groups, books, online educational materials, a medical professional, or a therapist. Reaching out for support may feel vulnerable and scary for survivors. When we push folks to get support before they are ready, it might slow the healing process.

If your partner has started seeking support from others, you can support them by validating any emotions they have during their interactions with others that they share with you. If they feel discounted, dismissed, or invalidated during the process of seeking support, try not to dismiss these feelings. Instead, acknowledge that it sucks when we don't feel heard or supported by people we are reaching out to for support. In this phase, you can also ask them whether they would like you to support them in any way as they seek help (for example, transportation, your presence, looking for resources for them).

Integrating Their Survivor Story

Through the support of others and self-reflection, many survivors are able to integrate the story of their sexual trauma experience into their lives. This does not mean that they deny the reality that they have experienced sexual assault, but that the event is no longer constantly at the forefront of their minds. They return to activities and relationships that bring them joy and feel more present in their life.

You can support your partner in this stage by continuing to practice positive relationship skills and boundaries explored in this book. Even when a survivor reaches this phase, they can become triggered. That is normal, and it can be helpful to let them know that it's okay and normal to experience trauma reactions. You can support your partner with tips from this book or by helping them seek the support they request.

Connecting to Others and Advocacy

When a survivor feels secure enough after their trauma healing, they may reach what I see as the final stage of healing: sharing their story with others and/or supporting advocacy efforts to change rape culture. They might volunteer with advocacy groups, attend marches and rallies, or share their story with others person-to-person, at events, or even online. Through the sharing of their stories, many survivors feel empowered and less alone.

You can support your partner in this phase by asking them whether they need emotional support before or after sharing their story with others. Even after years of healing, sharing their trauma story is a vulnerable and emotional experience. You might even choose to share your own experience and become an advocate yourself! If that is the case, there is more information on how you can do so later in this chapter.

Therapeutic Support for Trauma Survivors

When your partner is in the seeking support phase of their healing, they might be overwhelmed about where to start. There are many different modalities of therapeutic treatment and alternative treatments that can be supportive to folks. This section includes information on psychotherapeutic modalities and alternative therapies that you and your partner can review to help them identify what kind of support they feel more comfortable exploring.

Traditional Talk Therapy

Talk therapy is what most people first think about when they think of therapy or see therapy sessions in a TV show or movie. During talk therapy, you acknowledge and explore your experiences (past and present), and you may find a deeper understanding for yourself, which can lead to a decrease of your trauma symptoms and a more fulfilling life.

When it comes to sexual trauma, talk therapy can be incredibly useful. In our society, we tend to view sex (especially traumatic sexual experiences) with shame or awkwardness. This can cause us to refrain from talking about our trauma and stall the healing process. Talk therapy helps get this conversation going, and a skilled therapist will help you integrate your experience and move forward in your life.

Trauma-Informed Integrative Therapy

The primary focus of trauma-informed therapy is the impact of the trauma on the client's life; a trauma-informed therapist is trained to recognize trauma symptoms and conduct therapy at a pace that limits retraumatization of a survivor. This type of therapy is helpful because it can be personalized and modified to match the needs of each individual. Many therapists practice from an integrative perspective, meaning they integrate various methods into their therapy. You can ask them directly which modalities or styles of therapy they most often pull from to give you a clearer idea of what to expect.

Trauma-informed psychotherapy may include:
- eye movement desensitization and reprocessing (EMDR) therapy
- trauma-focused cognitive behavioral therapy (TF-CBT)
- somatic experiencing therapy
- brainspotting therapy
- sex therapy
- couples/family therapy
- internal family systems therapy

Alternative Healing Modalities

If a survivor finds that talk therapy or the trauma-informed psychotherapies above are not a good fit, they may explore alternative healing modalities, such as:
- art therapy
- dance therapy
- trauma-informed yoga
- drama therapy
- bibliotherapy
- Reiki
- acupuncture

Realistically, your partner may find that a couple of these treatment options work well, or maybe none of these treatments really help. Remember, everyone is different, and just because art therapy works for someone does not mean it will work for someone else. The trick is finding which treatments (or combination of treatments) work for them and their healing journey.

How You Can Practice Allyship Through Advocacy

In the remainder of the book I will be sharing tips and stories from real survivors and their partners. First, I invited a survivor I've had the pleasure of knowing, Nisha, to write about how you can be an ally to survivors by connecting to others and challenging rape culture.

• How to Stand Up Against Rape Culture

From Nisha:
What is rape culture? When we raise our children in a society that constantly objectifies and degrades women, teaches our young men to be hypersexual, and perpetuates misogyny in school, the workplace, and everywhere else, it is no surprise that rape is the standard result. Men grow up feeling that women are there for them, that when a woman says no, she really means yes, and that even if they do something, they'll be forgiven because, well, "Boys will be boys."

This is what makes rape culture. This is why we keep seeing increases in movements to call out rape culture—like #MeToo, #GenerationEquality, #TimesUp, and #NiUnaMenos. Unfortunately, even with these movements and an increase in activism, rape culture is still incredibly prevalent in our society. But there are ways to challenge it and help change our society for the better.

Just like with any other cultural norm, standing up to rape culture can be incredibly difficult. This is not because there aren't enough people who want to make and see a change in the culture—there are many millions. Rather, it is because rape culture is so ingrained in our society and many people go along with it without even realizing it.

There are a number of things that go into rape culture, and without understanding them, it can be impossible to stop this mindset and social culture from affecting our future generations. Here, I am going to dive into some of the things that go into rape culture and how you can challenge them.

Address the Root Causes

As I mentioned above, rape culture has been ingrained in our society for a long time. Simply wanting it to end is not going to be enough to remove all of its negative effects on our society. Just like when you are removing a weed from your garden, you need to ensure that you get to the roots.

There are two primary root causes of rape culture: victim blaming, which was described earlier in the book, and toxic masculinity, which enables men to believe it's okay to be aggressive toward, and possessive of, women. I'll expand upon this below. Both of these ideas perpetuate the notion that the woman is the one to blame when she gets raped. Whether it is song lyrics like "I know you want it" from the song "Blurred Lines" (and many more songs just like it) or saying, "She was drunk" or "She was dressed like she wanted it," victim blaming and toxic masculinity are all around us. Without making an effort to address these root causes, rape culture will never end.

Practice Zero Tolerance

If you hear a rape joke or you see a coworker touch another in a way that makes the person uncomfortable, speak up. The unfortunate reality is that not enough of us speak up in these situations. We may feel that it is not our business or that the person already knows that what they did was wrong. More often than not, when people get away with these jokes or acts of harassment, they think that it is okay to continue doing them.

We cannot let these things slide; it only perpetuates rape culture and validates (even if you do not mean to) individuals who sexually harass, assault, and rape others.

Redefine Masculinity

I mentioned the idea of "toxic masculinity" above, and for most of our society, there is no "masculinity" outside of the narrow view of toxic masculinity. This is because men grow up in a society that tells them that they need to be strong, not cry, make money for their families, and even be aggressive in their sexuality and possessive of the women in their lives.

But this is not good masculinity. This is putting all the societal pressure on men and telling them that women are there for them to interact with as they please. This is ingraining a sense of superiority in men at a young age that dramatically impacts their view of the world (and women) even without them noticing. It needs to end.

Now, even if you grew up with these values being constantly shoved in your face, you can still make a change. Think critically about what good masculinity means to you. Find out what the important characteristics of masculinity are to you and highlight those—rather than what our society has told you makes a "man."

Enthusiastic Consent

Many of us grew up hearing that a woman is playing "hard to get" or that sometimes women say no when they actually mean yes. These concepts are incredibly dangerous and harmful to women all over the world because when they tell a man no, he often assumes that he just hasn't charmed her quite enough yet. Of course, this does not only apply to women, and it is not only men who ignore the word "no." However, from a societal standpoint and in the lens of rape culture, it is far more common for men to ignore the "no" and continue pursuing a woman who does not want to be pursued.

This is where we need to make the shift. Rather than teaching our young boys that no can mean yes, we need to teach them to look for enthusiastic consent. Teach them to only move forward if their partner is enthusiastic about what is happening. Rape culture depends on victim blaming, and focusing on enthusiastic consent is an effective way to make pointing fingers at the victim's "unclear message" incredibly difficult.

Listen to Survivors

When someone comes out and tells you of their experience, you need to listen. One, it was probably incredibly challenging for them to bring it up and tell you about the traumatic experience they had to go through—especially if they are someone close to you. Two, they went through a traumatic experience that most members of society are likely to blame them for. They need your support, and you need to realize just how common sexual assault is in our society.

Educate the Next Generation

The newest generation (Generation Alpha) is currently being taught many of the same ideas that we were taught as children—both in school and through societal norms. If we want to change our trajectory and really get rid of rape culture, we need to start with how we raise our children. Help educate them about what is wrong with rape culture and how they can stand up against it.

Respect their choices in their lives and teach them about enthusiastic consent from a young age. Remember, consent can be for any type of situation. For example, maybe your child does not like being hugged (or maybe they do, just only by certain people or not all of the time). You can use this as a way to help them learn about consent and that their body is their own. Ask before you hug them or hold their hand. Encourage your other family members to do the same. This teaches your child that they are in control of their body and no one is entitled to touch it if they don't want them to.

Tips from Survivors and Their Partners

And now, to offer hope and insights from others walking the same path you are on, I'd like to share some words from actual survivors and partners who have each done multiple years of healing and relationship building. Please read on to see how they responded to questions I posed.

If a sexual trauma survivor's partner said to you, "I want to learn how to better support my partner," what would you tell them?

I would suggest creating a safe space with their partner's input and perspective.

This may look like reading up on sexual trauma, engaging in sensitive and affirming discussions with their partner, taking things at their partner's pace, and having patience as their partner learns to find safety and joy in sex again.

—AB, *Survivor*

I think the main things to consider when trying to support a trauma survivor are patience and understanding. Recovering from a trauma is definitely possible, but it is a very slow process that can be filled with setbacks and frustration. Having patience with your partner is the best way to support them. Understanding that their behavior and limitations are a result of their trauma and not necessarily who they are or how they want to be will help give you a better perspective. Your partner may be scared of things that you would not consider scary, or uncomfortable with situations that you don't think would be uncomfortable. Understanding why they are scared or uncomfortable helps you empathize with their feelings and help them to either work through their feelings or avoid the situations altogether. Communication is immensely helpful in situations like these. It's important to have an open dialogue for your partner to tell

you when something is scary or uncomfortable and to discuss whether this is something they are comfortable working through or whether the situation should be avoided. For example, my partner is very easily startled when I come home. We had a conversation about what we could do about it and found that it was more a matter of seeing me without knowing I was there, rather than me coming home unexpectedly. I made it a point to enter the house loudly and announce that I was home to make sure that she knew I was there. As it became a habit, I startled her only once or twice a month instead of daily.
—AW, *Partner of a Survivor*

I want to emphasize that a partner just taking the step to ask how they can be a support is being supportive. A significant number of people would never even ask and certainly wouldn't pick up a book.

Patience and communication. Be willing and able to provide the space for your partner when they want to talk about their trauma and how it affects them.

Be accepting of what your partner tells you. Listen when they say something is uncomfortable or triggering. Sometimes it may not make sense—be accepting anyway. Reassure your partner without discounting their trauma and feelings. Don't try to "fix"—just listen (unless asked by your partner).

—*TL, Survivor*

I would let them know I appreciate their interest and willingness to understand. I would also share with them some things I have learned about my trauma, such as examples of my triggers and red flags they should be made aware of, especially if I need help identifying responses I may not be attuned to when I am triggered. I would also encourage my partner to ask lots of questions. Let them know having an open, informal conversation, with a safe space to learn, is important for our relationship. At the end of the day, I want to support my partner's interests/concerns/questions while establishing a balanced learning environment because we all gain knowledge differently.

—*CG, Survivor*

Everyone is different, so listen to your partner and what they need. Understand their boundaries and expectations, but also be clear about your own. They might have a hard time trusting you—they might test you to see whether you are trustworthy. They do this to feel safe.

—*R, Survivor*

What has been challenging in building relationships with a sexual trauma survivor or a partner of a sexual trauma survivor?

Learning to trust. Unfortunately, those who cross our most important boundaries are often those we know very well—people we thought we could trust. This element adds to the trauma layers of betrayal and disillusionment.

—AB, *Survivor*

Being able to put into words what happened to me and finding trust in a partner with whom I can share my trauma. Also, battling my own demons of not wanting to place a heavy burden on someone I care about, especially knowing secondary trauma is a reality for many survivors' loved ones. As a survivor, you can't always know how your story might impact others, so there are times when finding the right balance of what exactly should be shared is quite challenging.

—CG, *Survivor*

While patience and understanding are very helpful in supporting a partner with trauma, establishing and maintaining your own personal boundaries and expectations are the hardest part of building a strong relationship. Establishing boundaries and expectations are a difficult part in any relationship, but it is even more challenging in a relationship with a trauma survivor. Trauma survivors may be uncomfortable or unwilling to fulfill your expectations due to their experiences; they may also have coping behaviors that are destructive, unhealthy, or unacceptable to you. There is a lot of frustration that comes with having your own needs unfulfilled or tolerating your partner's behaviors that you feel are intolerable. Communication is very important in situations like these, but if your partner is unable to compromise, being true to your own boundaries and expectations is important to your own health and happiness.

There is a lot of conflict in this choice—to potentially end the relationship, or adjust your expectations or boundaries. In my own personal example, my partner had a problem with substance abuse. She would become aggressive, abusive, and reckless when she drank. The substance abuse was mainly a mechanism to cope with her trauma, and she would rarely even remember what she did, but the behavior was not something I could continue to tolerate in the relationship. It was a tough situation for both of us—either she loses her main coping mechanism, I continue to tolerate an abusive partner, or we end the relationship. Through a lot of communication, hardship, and trial and error, she decided to stop drinking altogether, which was a very difficult thing for her, but we are both much happier.

—AW, *Partner of a Survivor*

Communication—figuring out how to share, what to share, trying not to over- or underread my partner's reactions, trying to figure out my triggers and explain them to my partner (especially when they don't make sense in my own head or feel silly). Sometimes something isn't triggering one day, but is the next. It's confusing at times for me, let alone for my partner, who can't read my thoughts.

Reframing intimacy—trying to rationalize within myself how something connected to my trauma can also be something that connects me to my partner. This is probably what I still struggle with the most. The desire to be fully present in the moment mixed with the fear of reacting or becoming anxious is difficult, but knowing my partner is aware that I might get triggered and is also able to be there for me if I do helps calm my fears. We have had numerous conversations about what I need in those moments (often assisted in these conversations by my lovely therapist), which allows him to be prepared for when it comes up.

Before we had these conversations, I would try to suppress the anxiety and it would end up with me having a full-blown panic attack. Now, I feel comfortable expressing discomfort during (or even before) something I am finding triggering in the moment. This is much easier for both of us—but has taken A LOT of trial and error.

—TL, *Survivor*

It's been hard when people have made assumptions about me based on my trauma. If a partner assumes that I like what I like sexually or that I am queer because of my trauma—that isn't true for me. My sexuality, desires, and identity are part of me and I don't want those things tied to my trauma.

—R, *Survivor*

What has been hopeful or helpful in building relationships with others as a sexual trauma survivor or with your trauma survivor partner?

Patience, sensitivity, and respect from both others and myself. While it hurts my heart to hear that others have undergone the same traumas, knowing that I am not alone brings me a sense of comfort in that we can empower each other as we heal.

—AB, *Survivor*

Communication has definitely been the most helpful part of building a strong relationship with my partner. Hearing from her that she wants to be better and knowing what she is working on to get better have been very inspiring. Seeing small changes over time with the things she says she's working on gives us both hope. I found it important to keep the mindset that my partner is doing the best that she can to heal from her trauma and make both of our lives better and happier. Communication helps me know what she's working on, how I can help, and what her goals are. With that insight I can be a better partner for her, and in turn she can be a better partner for me.

—AW, *Partner of a Survivor*

Having a supportive person. I get frustrated when I get triggered. Sometimes I get angry or sad. Having a partner who can support me through that, not be offended or take it as something against them, and accept that these emotions are present has been key to developing a deeper intimate relationship.

My partner and I have, in several ways, had to work our lives around my trauma and PTSD. It took me a long time to realize this wasn't "asking too much" of my partner. A small accommodation to hopefully get rid of a big source of stress.

For some people, having a partner who stomps his feet loudly up the stairs would be disruptive or frustrating. For me, it's an act of love. He knows that I startle very easily and I startle significantly less to a loud noise than to him suddenly appearing. So, he stomps as he's walking up to our house. I've noticed he does it when we are walking up to the house together, too—it's part of his routine now. This was something that was a huge struggle when we first moved into our house. And in less than a year, it is something we rarely think about but has made a huge difference for both of us. A seemingly simple thing made such an impact on my security.

Trusting my partner is crucial. Being able to tell my partner when I'm anxious and my partner respecting whether I want to talk about it or not. And knowing my partner can reassure me in those moments is so helpful.

—TL, *Survivor*

Finding what works best for my partner and me, by getting help with the trauma and the array of symptoms that stem from it. For me, that has been going to therapy and discovering comfortable ways to properly inform my partner of my past and of the ever evolving triggers I experience. Especially when it comes to being intimate with my partner, so they know what is safe and within the realm of what I am able to handle. And in return, what their needs are and how I am able to meet those needs without being compromised or put in a position where either my partner or I feel guilt for crossing an unknown line. Thus, having clear communication and boundaries brings a lot of hope and excitement.

—CG, *Survivor*

It can be hard to open up to a new partner—sharing the trauma again and taking the risk to trust again. Each time a relationship ends, it's like, *Do I want to do this again?* If I feel discarded, played, or disrespected by a partner, I'm easily triggered. When someone does respect my boundaries and my needs, and communicates their own stuff too, it's much more likely we'll be able to build a relationship.

—R, *Survivor*

What has been key to your healing and connection?

The key to my healing has been my own therapy work, connecting with my body (exercising, yoga, mindfulness), setting boundaries, and surrounding myself with people who respect the boundaries I set for myself. My partner has been instrumental in my healing process as well, as his understanding, patience, and love create a safe space for me. I am no longer afraid to grow where I once felt stunted; such is the power of secure love.

—AB, *Survivor*

Again, communication is the key to our connection. We encourage each other to talk about anything that's going on with each other or ourselves. Open communication helps us resolve our disagreements and disappointments, share our goals, and celebrate our successes. My partner's small successes also help us keep our connection strong. Knowing that she's getting better and living happier gives us both hope for the future. Healing from trauma is hard, and being a survivor's partner is hard as well. We've had big successes and big setbacks, but communicating well and celebrating our progress has been vital to sticking together.

—AW, *Partner of a Survivor*

Patience—both from my partner and with myself. Even this far in my healing journey, there are many days I struggle with it. I know there will be days in the future that I struggle with it. There are emotions with it that I don't always understand. And sometimes when I'm struggling, it's just inconvenient. In those moments, I have to stop and remember how far I've come in my healing journey. And remind myself that if I hadn't had patience with myself in those early, incredibly dark days, I definitely wouldn't have made it this far.

—*TL, Survivor*

Knowing you are not alone and are not something that needs to be fixed. Making the time and putting in the effort to build a strong support network for yourself. The trauma is and will always be a part of you, whether it be good or bad. And lastly, finding a way to accept and live with the trauma by grieving what was lost.

—*CG, Survivor*

Putting It All Together

As you can see, when reflecting on their own experiences, these survivors and partners touch on many of the themes we discussed in this book: communication, boundaries, empathy, understanding each other's triggers, taking things slowly, exploring sex together, and practicing good self-care. The healing these folks have had and that you will have doesn't happen overnight, but it is possible and can be so rewarding.

You've learned so much in this book! Are you able to look at your partner with more empathy? Are you starting to decrease your own stress and speak compassionately to yourself to get you through the hard moments? Do you have the relationship skills to get through cycles of disconnection and trauma triggers? Have you started to practice creating some of the bonding moments described in some of the relationship exercises? This book will always be here for you as you practice and integrate these skills, as I know you will.

In the introduction of this book, I made a bold assertion: that by supporting your survivor partner and improving your relationship, you will be changing the world. And this is something I truly believe happens when we understand what we've learned in this book and bring these concepts into our lives. Healthy relationships and support for survivors challenges rape culture and changes the world. You have a part in that! Thank you.

Acknowledgments

I wouldn't have been able to write a book for partners of sexual trauma survivors without the support of my own partner, Eric. *"...and you, a win-drose, a compass, my direction, my description of the world."*—Ian Burham.

Thank you to my amazing team of relationship and trauma therapists at Love Heal Grow therapy center in Northern California (https://www.lovehealgrow.com). Thank you, Raayha Bhatti, for supporting me at the practice and in edits of the book. Thank you to my clients, each of whom has changed my life. Thank you to the survivors who made contributions to this book. has changed my life. Thank you to the survivors who made contributions to this book.

Thank you to my mentor, Stephanie Buehler, for believing in me and writing the foreword for this book.

Thank you to all of the complex and wonderful women in and out of my life, especially Lyndsey, Sydney, MacKenzie, Auntie Jill, Mom, Grandmama, Ann, Mariana, Jackie, and Margaret. And I can't forget Bob, the rest of the Leevers, or my Poppa.

Thank you to Wendy Millstine, Rona Bernstein, and the entire team at New Harbinger for bringing this book to the world.

Thank you to Zooey for loving me. I miss you every day.

Thank you to the love of my life, my daughter Cecilia. *Beautiful, beautiful, beautiful, beautiful Cece.*

References

American Psychiatric Association. 2022. *Diagnostic and Statistical Manual of Mental Disorders: DSM-5 TR.* 5th ed. Arlington, VA: American Psychiatric Association.

Bowlby, J., M.D. Ainsworth, M. Boston, and D. Rosenbluth. 1956. "Effects of Mother-Child Separation." *British Journal of Medical Psychology* 29: 169–201.

Johnson, S.M. 2015. "Emotionally Focused Couple Therapy," in *Clinical Handbook of Couple Therapy*, edited by A.S. Gurman, J.L. Lebow, and D.K. Snyder, 97–128. New York: The Guilford Press.

Masters, W.H., V.E. Johnson, and R.C. Kolodny. 1994. *Heterosexuality.* New York: HarperCollins.

Nagoski, E., and A. Nagoski. 2019. *Burnout: The Secret to Unlocking the Stress Cycle.* 1st ed. New York: Ballantine Books.

National Sexual Violence Resource Center. 2018. "Sexual Assault Statistics." https://www.nsvrc.org/statistics.

Neff, K.D. 2012. "The Science of Self-Compassion," in *Wisdom and Compassion in Psychotherapy: Deepening Mindfulness in Clinical Practice*, edited by C.K. Germer and R.D. Siegel, 79–92. New York: The Guilford Press.

Walker, P. 2013. *Complex PTSD: From Surviving to Thriving: A Guide and Map for Recovering from Childhood Trauma*. Lafayette, CA: Azure Coyote Publishing.

Megan Lara Negendank, LMFT, CST, is a licensed marriage and family therapist, and a certified sex therapist. She is founder of Love Heal Grow, a psychotherapy center in Northern California where she specializes in trauma-informed, relationship-focused psychotherapy for survivors of trauma and their partners. She has been featured as a relationship expert on PBS, NPR, and in *Sacramento Magazine*.

Foreword writer **Stephanie Buehler, PsyD, CST-S,** is a licensed psychologist, certified sex therapist and supervisor, and fellow of the International Society for the Study of Women's Sexual Health. She is author of *What Every Mental Health Professional Needs to Know About Sex*.

Real change is possible

For more than forty-five years, New Harbinger has published proven-effective self-help books and pioneering workbooks to help readers of all ages and backgrounds improve mental health and well-being, and achieve lasting personal growth. In addition, our spirituality books offer profound guidance for deepening awareness and cultivating healing, self-discovery, and fulfillment.

Founded by psychologist Matthew McKay and Patrick Fanning, New Harbinger is proud to be an independent, employee-owned company. Our books reflect our core values of integrity, innovation, commitment, sustainability, compassion, and trust. Written by leaders in the field and recommended by therapists worldwide, New Harbinger books are practical, accessible, and provide real tools for real change.

 newharbingerpublications

MORE BOOKS from
NEW HARBINGER PUBLICATIONS

ACT WITH LOVE, SECOND EDITION
Stop Struggling, Reconcile Differences, and Strengthen Your Relationship with Acceptance and Commitment Therapy

A MINDFULNESS-BASED STRESS REDUCTION CARD DECK

HEALTHY CONFLICT, HAPPY COUPLE
How to Let Go of Blame and Grow Stronger Together

THE DIALECTICAL BEHAVIOR THERAPY DIARY, SECOND EDITION
Monitoring Your Emotional Regulation Day by Day

THE BODY AWARENESS WORKBOOK FOR TRAUMA
Release Trauma from Your Body, Find Emotional Balance, and Connect with Your Inner Wisdom

RECLAIMING PLEASURE
A Sex Positive Guide for Moving Past Sexual Trauma and Living a Passionate Life

REVEAL PRESS
An Imprint of New Harbinger Publications

newharbingerpublications
1-800-748-6273 / newharbinger.com

(VISA, MC, AMEX / prices subject to change without notice)
Follow Us

Don't miss out on new books from New Harbinger.
Subscribe to our email list at **newharbinger.com/subscribe**

Did you know there are **free tools** you can download for this book?

Free tools are things like **worksheets**, **guided meditation exercises**, and **more** that will help you get the most out of your book.

You can download free tools for this book—whether you bought or borrowed it, in any format, from any source—from the New Harbinger website. All you need is a NewHarbinger.com account. Just use the URL provided in this book to view the free tools that are available for it. Then, click on the "download" button for the free tool you want, and follow the prompts that appear to log in to your NewHarbinger.com account and download the material.

You can also save the free tools for this book to your **Free Tools Library** so you can access them again anytime, just by logging in to your account! Just look for this button on the book's free tools page.

+ Save this to my free tools library

If you need help accessing or downloading free tools, visit **newharbinger.com/faq** or contact us at customerservice@newharbinger.com.

Back Cover Material

Support your partner while cultivating love, trust, and intimacy

Sexual trauma can have a lasting impact on both survivors *and* the people who love them. If your partner has experienced sexual trauma, they may struggle with anxiety, post-traumatic stress disorder (PTSD), depression, or addiction. They may also be triggered by intimate situations, leaving *you* feeling confused, overwhelmed, or unsure of how to best support them. This gentle guide will give you the tools you need to help nurture intimacy and trust, and cultivate a secure relationship.

In ***Loving Someone Who Has Sexual Trauma,*** you'll discover attachment-based communication skills and trauma-informed techniques to help you understand the full impact of your partner's experience, and ultimately improve your relationship in the here and now. You'll also learn how to avoid common triggers, de-escalate from conflict, and build a closer bond—emotionally and physically. If you're ready to move beyond fear, anger, and detachment to a thriving intimate relationship where you both can feel loved, safe, and connected, this book can help you get started today.

Megan Lara Negendank, LMFT, CST, is a licensed marriage and family therapist, and a certified sex therapist. She is founder of Love Heal Grow, a psychotherapy center in Northern California where she specializes in trauma-informed, relationship-focused psychotherapy for survivors of trauma and their partners.